SpringerBriefs in Rights-Based Approaches to Social Work

Series Editor
Shirley Gatenio Gabel

More information about this series at http://www.springer.com/series/11694

Shirley Gatenio Gabel

A Rights-Based Approach to Social Policy Analysis

 Springer

Shirley Gatenio Gabel
New York, NY, USA

ISSN 2195-9749   ISSN 2195-9757   (electronic)
SpringerBriefs in Rights-Based Approaches to Social Work
ISBN 978-3-319-24410-5   ISBN 978-3-319-24412-9   (eBook)
DOI 10.1007/978-3-319-24412-9

Library of Congress Control Number: 2016931212

This Springer imprint is published by Springer Nature
The registered company is Springer International Publishing AG Switzerland

To my paternal grandparents and aunts who I never met because their lives were taken too soon and inhumanely.
To my maternal grandparents and parents whose survival is a beacon of strength, everyday.
To my husband, Ken, and daughter, Estee, who are my dreams realized.
Together they shine the light to a better world in which human rights live for all.

Foreword

Even though you and I are in different boats, you in your boat and we in our canoe, we share the same River of Life.

—Chief Oren Lyons, Onandaga Nation, USA

The rights of every man are diminished when the rights of one man are threatened.

—John F. Kennedy, Civil Rights Announcement, June 11, 1963

For over a century, social workers have worked to improve the lives and situations of individuals, families, and communities. Social workers, often acting on behalf of the state's interests, typically intervened according to what they themselves perceived to be deficits in the lives and behaviors of persons in need. This approach to working with people patronizes, stigmatizes, and too often revictimizes those we seek to assist. It is long past time to revitalize and reframe our approach to working with those we seek to serve. The books in this series reframe deficit models used by social work practitioners and instead propose a human rights perspective. Rights-based social work shifts the focus from human needs to human rights and calls on social workers and the populations they work with to actively participate in decision-making processes of the state so that the state can better serve the interests of the population. The authors in the series share their strategies for empowering the populations and individuals we, as social workers, engage with as clinicians, community workers, researchers, and policy analysts.

The roots of social work in the United States can be traced to the pioneering efforts of upperclass men and women who established church-based and secular charitable organizations that sought to address the consequences of poverty, urbanization, and immigration. These were issues that were ignored by the public sphere at the time. Little in the way of training or methods was offered to those who volunteered their resources, efforts, and time in these charitable organizations until later in the nineteenth century when concepts derived from business and industry were applied to distribution of relief efforts in what became known as "scientific charity."

This scientific approach led to the use of investigation, registration, and supervision of applicants for charity, and in 1877, the first American Charity Organization Society (COS) was founded in Buffalo, New York. The popularity of the approach grew quickly across the country. COS leaders wanted to reform charity by including an agent's investigation of the case's "worthiness" before distributing aid because they believed that unregulated and unsupervised relief led to more calls for relief.

Around the same time, an alternative response to the impact of industrialization and immigration was introduced and tested by the settlement house movement. The first US settlement, the Neighborhood Guild in New York City, was established in 1886, and less than three years later, Jane Addams and Ellen Gates Starr founded Hull House in Chicago, which came to symbolize the settlement house movement in the United States. Unlike the individually oriented COS, the settlement house movement focused on the environmental causes of poverty, seeking economic and social reforms for the poor and providing largely immigrant and migrant populations with the skills needed to stake their claims in American society.

The settlement house movement spread rapidly in the United States and by 1910, there were more than 400 settlements (Trolander, 1987; Friedman & Friedman, 2006). Advocacy for rights and social justice became an important component of the settlement activities and led to the creation of national organizations like the National Consumers' League, Urban League, Women's Trade Union League, and the National Association for the Advancement of Colored People (NAACP). The leaders of the movement led major social movements of the period, including women's suffrage, peace, labor, civil rights, and temperance, and were instrumental in establishing a federal-level children's bureau in 1912, headed by Julia Lathrop from Hull House.

During this same period, the charity organization societies set to standardize the casework skills for their work with individuals. Their methods became a distinct area of practice and were formalized as a social work training program in 1898 known as the New York School of Philanthropy and eventually, the Columbia University School of Social Work. In 1908, the Chicago Commons offered a full curriculum through the Chicago School of Civics and Philanthropy (now the University of Chicago's School of Social Service Administration) based on the practices and principles of the settlement movement. By 1919, there were 17 schools of social work.

Efforts already underway to secure and strengthen pragmatically derived casework knowledge into a standardized format were accelerated following Abraham Flexner's provocative lecture in 1915 questioning whether social work was a profession because he believed it lacked specificity, technical skills, or specialized knowledge (Morris, 2008). By the 1920s, casework emerged as the dominant form of professional social work in the United States and remained primarily focused on aiding impoverished children and families but was rapidly expanding to work with veterans and middle-class individuals in child guidance clinics.

As social work branched out to other populations, it increasingly focused on refining clinical treatment modalities and over time clinical work too often stood apart from community work, advocacy, and social policy. Although social work education standards today require all students to be exposed to clinical and casework, community practice, advocacy, research and policy, most schools do not prioritize the integrated practice of these areas in the advanced year of social work education (Austin & Ezell, 2004; Knee & Folsom, 2012).

Despite the development of sophisticated methods for helping others, social work practice overly relies on charity and needs-based approaches. These approaches are built on the deficit model of practice in which professionals or individuals with greater means diagnose what is "needed" in a situation and the "treatment" or services required to yield the desired outcome that has been set by the profession or other persons of advantage. Judgments of need are based on professional research, practice wisdom, and theory steeped in values (Ife, 2012). These values, research, theories, and practices typically reflect the beliefs of the persons pronouncing judgment, not necessarily the values and theories of the person who is being judged. This has the effect of disempowering and diminishing control of one's own life while privileging professionals (Ife, 2012). In turn, this risks reinforcing passiveness and perpetuating the violation of rights among the marginalized populations we seek to empower and at best maintains the status quo in society.

Needs-based approaches typically arise from charitable intentions. In social welfare, charity-based efforts have led to the labeling of persons worthy and unworthy of assistance, attributing personal behaviors as the cause of marginalization, poverty, disease, and disenfranchisement, and restricted the types of aid available accordingly. Judgments are cast by elites regarding who is deserving and who is not based on criteria that serve to perpetuate existing social, economic, and political relationships in charity-based approaches. Needs-based approaches attempt to introduce greater objectivity into the process of selecting who is helped and how by using evidence to demonstrate need and introducing effective and efficient interventions to improve the lot of the needy and society as a whole. Yet the solutions of needs-based efforts like charity-based ones are laden with the values of professionals and the politically elite and do not necessarily reflect the values and choices of the persons who are the object of assistance. Needs-based approaches prioritize the achievement of professionally established goals over the process of developing the goals, and, too often, the failure of outcomes is attributed to personal attributes or behaviors of individuals or groups who receive assistance. For example, the type of services a person diagnosed with a mental disorder receives in a needs-based approach will be often decided by authorities or experts according to their determination of what is best for the person and is likely to assume that a person with a mental disorder is incapable of making choices or at least not "good" choices. Programmatic success would then be evaluated according to adherence to the treatment plan prescribed by the persons with authority in the situation and may omit consumers' objections or own assessments of well-being.

Unlike needs-based and charity-based approaches, a rights-based approach places equal value on process and outcome. In rights based work, goals are temporary markers that are adjusted as people perpetually re-evaluate and understand rights in new ways calling for new approaches to social issues. For example, having nearly achieved universal access to primary education, a re-evaluation of the right to education might lead to a new goal to raise the quality of education or promote universal enrollment in secondary education among girls. Rights-based approaches are anchored in a normative framework that are based in a set of internationally agreed upon legal covenants and conventions, which in and of themselves can provide a different and potentially more powerful approach. A key aspect of this approach posits the right of all persons to participate in societal decision making, especially those persons or groups whom are affected by the decisions. For example, Article 12 of the United Nations Convention on the Rights of the Child (UNCRC) asserts that states "shall assure to the child who is capable of forming his or her own views the right to express those views freely in all matters affecting the child, the views of the child being given due weight in accordance with the age and maturity of the child" (UNCRC, 1989). Likewise, the preamble to the United Nations Convention on the Rights of Persons with Disabilities (UNCRPD) holds states responsible for "redressing the profound social disadvantage of persons with disabilities and (to) promote their participation in the civil, political, economic, social, and cultural spheres with equal opportunities" (UNCRPD, 2006).

A rights-based approach requires consideration of the universally recognized principles of human rights: the equality of each individual as a human being, the inherent dignity of each person and the rights to self-determination, peace and security. Respect for all human rights sets the foundation for all civil, political, social, and economic goals that seek to establish certain standards of well-being for all persons. Rights-based efforts remove the charity dimension by recognizing people not only as beneficiaries, but as active rights holders.

One of the areas of value added by the human rights approach is the emphasis it places on the *accountability* of policy makers and other actors whose actions have an impact on the rights of people. Unlike needs, rights imply duties, and duties demand accountability (UN OHCHR 2002: paragraph 23). Whereas needs may be met or satisfied, rights are realized and as such must be respected, protected, facilitated, and fulfilled. Human rights are indivisible and interdependent and unlike needs that can be ranked, all human rights are of equal importance. A central dynamic of a rights-based approach is thus about identifying root causes of social issues and empowering rights holders to understand and if possible claim their rights while duty bearers are enabled to meet their obligations. Under international law, the state is the principal duty bearer with respect to the human rights of the people living within its jurisdiction. However, the international community at large also has a responsibility to help realize universal human rights. Thus, monitoring and accountability procedures extend beyond states to global actors—such as the donor community, intergovernmental organizations, international non-governmental organizations (NGOs) and transnational corporations—whose actions bear upon the enjoyment of human rights in any country (UN OHCHR, 2002: paragraph 230).

Table 1 summarizes the differences between charity-, needs-, and rights-based approaches.

It can be argued that rights-based practice is not strikingly different from the way many social workers practice. For example, the strengths perspective that has become a popular approach in social work practice since the 1990s focuses on

Table 1 Comparison of charity-, needs-, and rights-based approaches to social issues

	Charity-based	Needs-based	Rights-based
Goals	Assistance to deserving and disadvantaged individuals or populations to relieve immediate suffering	Fulfilling an identified deficit in individuals or community through additional resources for marginalized and disadvantaged groups	Realization of human rights that will lead to the equitable allocation of resources and power
Motivation	Religious or moral imperative of rich or endowed to help the less fortunate who are deserving of assistance	To help those deemed in need of help so as to promote well-being of societal members	Legal obligation to entitlements
Accountability	May be accountable to private organization	Generally accountable to those who identified the need and developed the intervention	Governments and global bodies such as the donor community, intergovernmental organizations, international NGOs, and transnational corporations
Process	Philanthropic with emphasis on donor	Expert identification of need, its dimensions, and strategy for meeting need within political negotiation. Affected population is the object of interventions	Political with a focus on participatory process in which individuals and groups are empowered to claim their rights
Power relationships	Preserves status quo	Largely maintain existing structure, change might be incremental	Must change
Target population of efforts	Individuals and populations worthy of assistance	Disadvantaged individuals or populations	All members of society with an emphasis on marginalized populations
Emphasis	On donor's benevolent actions	On meeting needs	On the realization of human rights
Interventions respond to	Immediate manifestation of problems	Symptomatic deficits and may address structural causes	Fundamental structural causes while providing alleviation from symptomatic manifestations

strengths, abilities, and potential rather than problems, deficits, and pathologies (Chapin, 1995; Early & GlenMaye, 2000; Saleebey, 1992a) and "interventions are directed to the uniqueness, skills, interests, hopes, and desires of each consumer, rather than a categorical litany of deficits" (Kisthardt, 1992: 60–61). In the strengths-based approach, clients are usually seen as the experts on their own situation and professionals are understood as not necessarily having the "best vantage point from which to appreciate client strengths" (Saleebey, 1992b, p. 7). The focus is on "collaboration and partnership between social workers and clients" (Early & GlenMaye, 2000: 120).

The strengths perspective has provided a way for many social workers to engage themselves and the populations they work with in advocacy and empowerment that builds upon capabilities and more active processes of social change. Indeed, strengths-based and rights-based approaches build upon the strengths of individuals and communities and both involve a shift from a deficit approach to one that reinforces the potential of individuals and communities. Both approaches acknowledge the unique sets of strengths and challenges of individuals and communities and engage them as partners in developing and implementing interventions to improve well-being giving consideration to the complexities of environments. However, the strengths-based perspective falls short of empowering individuals to claim their rights within a universal, normative framework that goes beyond social work to cut across every professional discipline and applies to all human beings. Rights-based approaches tie social work practice into a global strategy that asserts universal entitlements as well as the accountability of governments and other actors who bear responsibility for furthering the realization of human rights.

The link between social work and human rights normative standards is an important one as history has repeatedly demonstrated. In many ways, social work has been moving toward these standards (Healy, 2008) but has yet to fully embrace it. Social work has been a contradictory and perplexing profession functioning both to help and also to control the disadvantaged. At times social workers have engaged in roles that have furthered oppression (Ife, 2012) and served as a "handmaiden" to those who seek to preserve the status quo (Abramovitz, 1998, p. 512). Social benefits can be used to integrate marginalized populations but also be used to privilege and exclude, particularly when a charity-based approach is utilized. When conditional, benefits can also be used as a way to modify behaviors and as a means of collecting information on private individual and family matters.

This contradictory and perplexing role of social work is shown albeit, in an extreme case, by social work involvement in the social eugenics movement specifically promulgated by National Socialists leaders in the 1930s and 1940s (Johnson & Moorehead, 2011). Leading up to and during World War II, social workers were used as instruments to implement Nazi policies in Europe. Though the history of social work and social work education is different in each European country, in at least Germany, Austria, Switzerland, Czechoslovakia, and Hungary, authorities used social workers to exclude what the state considered at the time to be undesirable populations from assistance, to reward those who demonstrated loyalty and pledged to carry forth the ideology of the state, and to collect information on personal and family affairs for the state (Hauss & Schulte, 2009). University-based and other forms of social work training were closed down in Germany in 1933 when the National Socialists assumed control because welfare was regarded as superfluous and a "waste for persons useless to the national community" (*Volksgemeinschaft* as quoted in Hauss & Schulte, 2009, p. 9). "Inferiors" were denied support and social workers were re-educated in Nazi ideology to train mothers on how to raise children who were loyal and useful to the ambitions of the National Socialists (Kruse, 2009). Similarly in Hungary, where social workers were referred to as "social sisters," social workers were re-educated to train mothers about the value of their contributions to the state (mainly their reproductive capacity and rearing of strong children for the state) and were instrumental in the implementation of Hungary's major welfare program that rewarded "worthy" clients with the redistribution of assets from Jewish estates (Szikra, 2009). As Szrika notes, "In the 1930s social policy and social work constituted a central part of social and economic policy-making that was fueled by nationalist and anti-Semitic ideology, influenced by similar practices in Germany, Italy and Czechoslavakia" (p. 116). Following Nazi ideological inoculation based on eugenics and race hate, social workers in Austria were charged with the responsibility of collecting incriminating information regarding mental illness, venereal disease, prostitution, alcoholism, hereditary diseases, and disabilities that would then be used to deny social benefits, prohibit marriages, and even select children for Austria's euthanasia program (Melinz, 2009).

Using social workers to realize state ideology was also employed to advance the Soviet agenda beginning in 1918 (Iarskaia-Smirnova & Romanov, 2009). The provision of social services was distributed across multiple disciplines among the helping professions and the term social work was not used because of its association to Western social welfare (Iarskaia-Smirnova & Romanov, 2009). These professionals, often referred to as social agents (workers in nurseries and youth centers, activists in women's organizations and trade unions, nurses, educators and domestic affairs officials), were charged with the double-task of social care and control. Early on social agents contributed to the establishment of standards designating worthy and unworthy behavior and activities and practices such as censure and social exclusion designed to alienate those who did not comply with state goals (Iarskaia-Smirnova & Romanov, 2009).

The use of social workers to carry out goals seemingly in contradiction of social work's ethics can be found in many examples in the United States as well (Abramovitz, 1998). In his book, *The Child Savers: The Invention of Delinquency* (1965), Anthony Platt demonstrates that despite well-intentioned efforts to protect youth, the establishment of the juvenile justice system in the United States removed youth from the adult justice systems and in doing so created a class of delinquents who were judged without due process. Platt argues that "child savers should in no sense be considered libertarians or humanists" (Platt, 1965, p. 176). The juvenile justice system that these reformers—many of who were social work pioneers—created in the United States purposefully blurred the distinction between delinquent and dependent young people. Labeling dependent children as delinquents, most of whom had committed no crime, robbed them of their opportunity to due process. The state and various religious organizations were given open reign to define delinquency as they saw fit and children who were perceived to be out of order or young women who were viewed as immoral were committed to institutions or other forms of state supervision with no means of redress.

More recently, Bumiller's analysis of domestic violence in the United States rouses our consciousness of the ways in which social workers engaged with persons involved in domestic violence and/or rape may inadvertently squash rather than empower individuals and families (Bumiller, 2008). Bumiller (2008) uses sexual violence to demonstrate how lawyers, medical professionals, and social workers may be contributing to passivity of social service beneficiaries and in doing so, enlarge the state's ability to control the behaviors of its members. As Bumiller explains, our public branding of perpetrators of sexual violence as deserving of severe punishment and isolation allow us then to deem them incapable of rehabilitation, and so we offer few opportunities for perpetrators to rejoin society as functioning members. In contrast, we expend resources toward "treating" victims to turn them into successful survivors and in the process of doing so instill their dependency on the state. We do this by requiring victims who seek support and protection from the state to comply with authorities, which in many cases are social workers, and acquiesce to the invasion of state control into their lives. In return for protection and assistance, needy women and children often relinquish control of their own lives and are forced to become individuals who need constant oversight and regulation. "As women have become the subjects of a more expansive welfare state, social service agencies have viewed women and their needs in ways that have often discouraged them from resisting regulations and from being active participants in their own decisions" (Bumiller, 2008). Some social workers use professional authority to support a deficit approach that allows social workers to scrutinize the parenting skills, education, housing, relationships, and psychological coping skills of those who have experienced sexual violence and then prescribe behaviors necessary to access to benefits. Those who voice complaints and resist scrutiny may be denied benefits such as disqualifying women from TANF benefits who fail to comply with work requirements or cutting off assistance to women who return to violent relationships. As key actors in this process, social workers have the opportunity to legitimize women's voice both within social welfare institutions and within the confines of relationships rather than reinforcing dependency and in some circumstances, revictimizing the individuals by making compliance a prerequisite for assistance.

The commonality of these examples lies in the omission of a normative frame that transcends national borders. The foundation of a rights-based approach is nested in universal legal guarantees to protect individuals and groups against the actions and omissions that interfere with fundamental freedoms, entitlements, and human dignity as first presented in the Universal Declaration of Human Rights (United Nations, 1948). International human rights law is based on a series of international conventions, covenants, and treaties ratified by states as well as other nonbinding instruments such as declarations, guidelines, and principles. Taken together these inalienable, interdependent, interrelated, and indivisible human rights are owned by people everywhere and responsibility to respect, protect, and fulfill these rights is primarily the obligation of the state.

Bonding social work practice to these international legal instruments obligates social workers to look beyond their own government's responses to social issues, to empower the populations they work with to have their voice heard, and to recast the

Table 2 Rights-based approaches to social work practice at different levels of intervention

Individuals seeking assistance are not judged to be worthy or unworthy of assistance but rather are viewed as rights holders. Social workers assist others in claiming their rights and helping others understand how individual rights have been violated. Interventions offered are not patronizing or stigmatizing, rather methods provide assistance based on the dignity of and respect for all individuals.
Example of individual-centered change: *Sexually trafficked persons are viewed as rights holders whose rights were violated rather than as criminals and are offered healing services and other benefits to restore their wholeness.*

Community/group/organization efforts are redirected away from proving that they deserve or need a resource toward learning about how they can claim their entitlements to resources. Social workers facilitate human rights education among group members including knowledge of human rights instruments, principles, and methods for accessing rights.
Example of group-centered change: *Groups are offered opportunities to learn about their housing rights, the change process in their community and learn skills so that they can claim their right to participation in community decision making.*

Society redirects its social policies and goals to facilitate the realization of human rights including addressing human needs. Macropracticing social workers affect the policy process and goals by expanding means for all members of a society to have their voices heard in the decision-making process.
Example of society-centered change: *Persons with disabilities are able to participate in the policy-making process through the use of technology that allows them to participate in meetings from their homes.*

neglected sovereignty of marginalized individuals and communities. It moves social workers away from being agents of the state to being change agents in keeping with the founding vision of social work. It reunites the different methods of social work practice by obligating all social workers to reflect on how public policies affect the rights of individuals and communities as well as how individual actions affect the rights of others (see Table 2). A rights-based approach compels social workers to look beyond existing methods of helping that too often exist to justify state intervention without addressing the root causes of the situation. It calls upon social workers who often act as agents of the state to acknowledge and act on their responsibility as moral duty bearers who have the obligation to respect, protect, and fulfill the rights of rights holders.

Rights-based approaches in social work have gained international acceptance in the past two decades more so outside of the United States than within. Social workers in the United States are relatively new to human rights practice, in part because of longstanding resistance known as "American exceptionalism" which allows the United States to initiate and even demand compliance of human rights abroad while repeatedly rejecting the application of international standards for human rights in the United States (Hertel & Libal, 2011). Most Americans are knowledgeable about civil and political rights, yet far fewer are as familiar with economic, social, and cultural rights. Relatively limited engagement in this area by social workers also stems from the perception that human rights activism is best led and achieved by lawyers or elite policy advocates. The books in this series are written to facilitate rights-based approaches to social work practice both in the United States and around the world and recognize that exposure to human rights multilateral treaties and applications may vary depending on where the reader was educated or trained.

A rights-based approach brings a holistic perspective with regards to civil, political, social, economic, and cultural roles we hold as human beings and a more holistic understanding of well-being that goes beyond the meeting of material needs. Our understanding of human rights is always evolving, and our methods, practices, research, interventions, and processes should evolve as our understanding deepens. The purpose of this series is to assist social work practitioners, educators, and students toward operationalizing a new approach to social work practice that is grounded in human rights. It is hoped that the books will stimulate discussion and the introduction of new methods of practice around maximizing the potential of individuals, communities, and societies. The books, like social work, reflect the wide range of practice methods, social issues, and populations while specifically addressing an essential area of social work practice. By using current issues as examples of rights-based approaches, the books facilitate the ability of social workers familiar with human rights to apply rights-based approaches in their practice. Each book in the series calls on social work practitioners in clinical, community, research, or policy-making settings to be knowledgeable about the laws in their jurisdiction but to also look beyond and hold states accountable to the international human rights laws and framework.

Fordham University, New York, NY   Shirley Gatenio Gabel

References

Abramovitz, M. (1998). Social work and social reform: An arena of struggle. *Social Work, 43* (6), 512–526.

Austin, M. J., & Ezell, M. (2004). Educating future social work administrators. *Administration in Social Work, 28* (1), 1–3.

Bumiller, K. (2008). *In an abusive state: How neoliberalism appropriated the feminist movement against sexual violence*. Durham: Duke University Press.

Chapin, R. (1995). Social policy development: The strengths perspective. *Social Work, 40* (4), 506–514.

Early, T., & GlenMaye, L. (2000). Valuing families: Social work practice with families from a strengths perspective. *Social Work, 45* (2), 118–130.

Friedman, M., & Friedman, B. (2006). *Settlement houses: Improving the welfare of America's immigrants*. New York: Rosen Publishing.

Hauss, G., & Schulte, D. (Eds.). (2009). *Amid social contradictions : Towards a history of social work in Europe*. Opladen, Farmington Hills, MI: Barbara Budrich Publishers.

Healy, L. M. (2008). Exploring the history of social work as a human rights profession. *International Social Work, 51* (6), 735–746.

Hertel, S. & Libal, K. (2011). *Human Rights in the United States: Beyond Exceptionalism*. Cambridge.

Iarskaia-Smirnova, E., & Romanov, P. (2009). Rhetoric and practice of modernisation: Soviet social policy (1917–1930). In G. Hauss & D. Schulte (Eds.), *Amid social contradictions: Towards a history of social work in Europe*. MI: Barbara Budrich Publishers.

Ife, J. (2012). *Human rights and social work : Towards rights-based practice*. Cambridge: Cambridge University Press.

Johnson, S., & Moorhead, B. (2011). Social eugenics practices with children in Hitler's Nazi Germany and the role of social work: Lessons for current practice. *Journal of Social Work Values and Ethics, 8* (1). http://www.jswve.org.

Kisthardt, W. (1992). A strengths model of case management: The principles and functions of a helping partnership with persons with persistent mental illness. In D. Saleebey (Ed.), *The strengths perspective in social work practice*. New York: Longman.

Knee, R. T., & Folsom, J. (2012). Bridging the crevasse between direct practice social work and management by increasing the transferability of core skills. *Administration in Social Work, 36,* 390–408.

Kruse, E. (2009). Toward a history of social work training Germany—discourses and struggle for power at the turning points. In G. Hauss & D. Schulte (Eds.), *Amid social contradictions: Towards a history of social work in Europe*. MI: Barbara Budrich Publishers.

Melinz, G. (2009). In the interest of children: Modes of intervention in family privacy in Austria (1914–1945). In G. Hauss & D. Schulte (Eds.), *Amid social contradictions: Towards a history of social work in Europe*. MI: Barbara Budrich Publishers.

Morris, P. M. (2008). Reinterpreting Abraham Flexner's speech, 'Is social work a profession?' Its meaning and influence on the field's early professional development. *Social Service Review, 82* (1), 29–60.

Platt, A. M. (1965). *The child savers: The invention of delinquency*. Chicago, IL: University of Chicago Press.

Saleebey, D. (1992a). Introduction: Beginnings of a strengths approach to practice. In D. Saleebey (Ed.), *The strengths perspective in social work practice*. New York: Longman.

Saleebey, D. (Ed.). (1992b). *The strengths perspective in social work practice*. New York: Longman.

Szikra, D. (2009). Social policy and anti-semitic exclusion before and during WW II in Hungary: The case of productive social policy. In G. Hauss & D. Schulte (Eds.), *Amid social contradictions: Towards a history of social work in Europe*. MI: Barbara Budrich Publishers.

Trolander, J. A. (1987). *Professionalism and social change: from the settlement house movement to neighborhood centers, 1886 to the present*. New York: Columbia University Press.

United Nations. (1948, December 9). *Convention on the prevention and punishment of genocide*. Retrieved from http://www.ohchr.org/EN/ProfessionalInterest/Pages/CrimeOfGenocide.aspx.

United Nations. (1989, November 20). *Convention on the rights of the child*. New York: United Nations. Retrieved from http://www2.ohchr.org/english/law/pdf/crc.pdf.

United Nations Office of the High Commissioner for Human Rights (UN OHCHR). (2002). Draft Guidelines for a Human Rights Approach to Poverty Reduction Strategies 2002.

United Nations. (2006, December 13). *Convention on the rights of persons with disabilities*. New York: United Nations. Retrieved from http://www2.ohchr.org/english/law/pdf/disabilitiesconvention.pdf.

Acknowledgements

In my journey of learning about human rights, I was fortunate to have a Human Rights family—that is a group of academics who shared an interest in human rights, theory, instruments and practice. We learned from and supported one another. Their work and their questions inspired me. Members came and went but at the core were Susan Mapp, Dennis Ritchie, Lynne Healy, Kathryn Libal, Megan Berthold, David Androff, and Jane McPherson. Thank you!

Greatest appreciation goes to my smart, fashionable, and pleasure to work with editor at Springer, Jennifer Hadley. HerQ1 support, guidance, and willingness to always celebrate our accomplishments refueled my commitment though out the series.

A special thanks to all the authors in the series. I learned from each of you and you have made all our lives a little better through your pioneering work on human rights.

Contents

Chapter 1
Understanding a Rights-Based Approach to Social Policy Analysis

"Policy analysis is more art than science" (Bardach, 2005, p. xiv).
    The study of public policy is "a mood more than a science, a loosely organized body of precepts and positions rather than a tightly integrated body of systematic knowledge, more art and craft than a genuine 'science'" (Moran, Goodin, & Rein, 2006, p. 5).

Social policies have the potential to play key roles in transforming our current societies into more equitable and just ones and yet we tend to fall back on implementing social policies that most resemble the ones we have, policies that far too often lack evidence of their effectiveness, and ones that value efficiency and development more than human dignity, freedom, equity, and equality, both in the process and outcomes.

1.1 Models of Social Policy Analysis

Policy analysis is the effort to systematically understand the consequences of public actions and intent on different sectors of society. Typically, the field is thought to originate in post-WWII military planning carried out by the RAND Corporation and other think tanks. Its intellectual roots are often cited to be Harold Lasswell's political analysis work beginning in the late 1940s and solidified by the formal development of cost benefit analysis in the 1950s. Policy analysis is interdisciplinary, drawing on concepts from economics, political science, sociology, public administration, and history.

Initially, policy analysis was used to better understand the strengths and limitations of policy options for the military and water resource issues and was extended to other fields over time. It was used in the late 1960s to understand the effects of health, education, and anti-poverty policies of Lyndon Johnson's Great Society and this type of study commonly became known as social policy.

© Springer International Publishing Switzerland 2016
S. Gatenio Gabel, *A Rights-Based Approach to Social Policy Analysis*,
SpringerBriefs in Rights-Based Approaches to Social Work,
DOI 10.1007/978-3-319-24412-9_1

Although social policy analysis has been practiced as a discipline for decades, its ability to produce intentional results continues to elude policymakers and analysts. Richard Nelson poignantly summarized this frustration in 1977, "If we can land a man on the moon, why can't we solve the problems of the ghetto? The question stands as a metaphor for a variety of complaints about the uneven performance of the American political economy. In an economy with such vast resources and powerful technologies, why can't we provide medical care at a reasonable cost to all who need it, keep the streets, air, and water clean, keep down crime, educate ghetto kids, provide decent and low-cost mass transport..." (Nelson, 1977).

A variety of frameworks on social policy analysis have been developed by social workers and scholars in related fields (Bardach, 1986; Chambers, 2000; DiNitto, 1995; Dobelstein, 1996; Gilbert & Terrell, 1986), each rooted in the rationalist approach initially embraced by social planners, each emphasizing a different aspect of analysis and intent of social policy and sometimes confounding the policy process with policy analysis. Policy analysis tends to consist of consideration of policy choices, evaluating the achievement of a policy goal, and sometimes the political, social, and technical processes in policy formulation (Stone, 2002, 2011). Rarely, however, do analyses account for policy choices, evaluation of selected goals, and the processes involved simultaneously—a departure from the generally more holistic approaches of social work practice. Social policy goals tend to be treated as finite ends, most often related to meeting unmet needs of a population. Often dominated by economics, policy analyses tend to favor efficiency over other values, driving these other "values underground, to make analysis appear more scientific by omitting certain basic assumptions from the discussion" (Myrdal, 1968) and in so doing confine social policy to rationality in decision making and its subsequent evaluations. Gilbert and Terrell (2005) argue that though less recognized, social values do underlie policy analyses and typically define the range of alternatives available and are embedded in the theories or assumptions justifying the choices.

The process of embedding these values is the least studied among researchers. Policies are often formulated and implemented at multiple levels of government sometimes reflecting the conflicts and differences in priorities and values at various levels of society. For example, federal policy may be funneled through state governments and implemented at local levels. Rather than focusing on better understanding the priorities at each level and its effect on policymaking and outcomes, most students of social policy analysis are taught to analyze the efficiency and effectiveness of implementation on meeting the policy goals of the policy engineers, neglecting to account for differences in priorities along the way.

This is interesting since the connection to a specific value orientation seems to have been at the core of the founding of policy analysis. Lasswell called for a development of the policy science of democracy—in other words, policy analysis would be used to further democratic values. As an applied social science, Lasswell intended for policy analysis to be used to diagnose societal missteps and recommend ways to get back on track at minimal cost and maximum societal gain (Smith & Larimer, 2009). Yet as Ingram and Smith have noted, policy analysis techniques are rarely created to measure ways in which citizenship and democracy can be fostered (1998).

"Rather than providing useful research questions about citizenship and democracy, existing frameworks and methods ignore normative questions about citizenship and democracy through which public policy scholars can assess contemporary institutional and policy changes" (Ingram & Smith, 1998, p. 1). In his later work, Lasswell makes clear that the policy process should not be sequestered among policy analysts and the administrative state; rather, it should be committed to the "encouragement of continuous general participation" (Lasswell, 1971, p. 117) and the aim of policy analysts should be "to subordinate the particular interests of a profession to the discovery and encouragement of public interest. This implies direct community participation as well as client service" (Lasswell, 1971, p. 119).

Not only do present policy analysis frameworks and methods too often neglect to assess the ability of current policies to further the goals of democracy but they also mask the purpose of policies by neglecting to assess the participatory process in the making of the policy. Although views on what constitutes a democracy vary widely, the ability of citizenry to participate in the decision-making process, equality, and accountability are often cited as key aspects of democracy (Bollen & Bollen, 2000; Sodaro, 2004)—yet few social policy analyses measure the increase in citizenry participation, equality, or accountability as a result of policy. Welfare reform in the United States in 1996 as embodied in the new welfare program, Temporary Assistance to Needy Families (TANF) is an example of this. According to Blank's extensive review of research conducted of the methodological techniques used to usher in and assess welfare reform in the 1990s, the analysis of public assistance programs historically focused on each state finding the point at which the benefits were low enough so as to encourage increased labor efforts (Blank, 2002). Because of the complexity of the program, its interrelationships with other benefit programs and state variations, researchers heavily relied on the analysis of single state and administrative data, which in of themselves create problems for generalizability and comparability. Absence from the literature is the voice of beneficiaries and their views about the welfare overhaul. One would think that beneficiaries, some of whom had extensive experiences with the system and its changes, would be able to contribute valuable information to be considered. The resulting reform is noted for its paternalism and conditionalities imposed on potential recipients. Beneficiaries deviating from the normative prescriptions established by the law face the possibility of fiscal sanctions and deepened struggles in caring for themselves and their children. Clearly, one of the intents of the reform was to steer individuals toward postponing child bearing until the age of majority, marriage, and employment. The standards established by the law however do not reflect that 41 % of all children in the United States are born outside of marriage (Martin, Hamilton, Osterman, Curtain, & Mathews, 2015). It seems unlikely then, if in true democratic spirit the opinions of all stakeholders including recipients and parents had been heard, that TANF as we know it, would be have been the outcome.

Our existing modes of policy analysis seem to embrace an instrumental focus that looks to answer how we can run society more effectively and efficiently and sidesteps the contentious and critical debates that might arise if we were to ask the beneficiaries themselves how they wanted to be helped and the values our policies should further. As a result, efficiency is elevated to an end, not a method of achieving an end. Efficiency however can have detrimental effects on democracy. It often conflicts with other highly valued social norms such as equity, participation, or justice.

Participatory involvement alone will not reorient public policies or the policymaking process. Policies need to be evaluated against the normative goals of a society that were arrived at through the participation of its broad spectrum of citizenry. Otherwise, policies can easily become instruments to effectively and efficiently implement the goals determined by an elite group that often omits the importance of negotiating and bargaining that occurs in policymaking. As Stone states, it is as though the scientific approach to public policy in effect became a mission to rescue "public policy from the irrationalities and indignities of politics (Stone, 2002, p. 7)." The problem being that public policy is very political and not particularly scientific, so choosing to pursue a strictly rational approach is much like burying one's head in sand and not confronting the value-laden realities of public policy. Instead, the policy process should be embracing normative theories as the gyroscope of policy studies (deLeon, 1997; Fischer, 2003; Stone, 2011).

One of the problems in performing policy analysis under the guise of objectivity using the rational model approach is that the goals are treated as though they are value-free when in fact they are not and as Lasswell himself indicates, they were never intended to be (Lasswell & Lerner, 1951). Limiting policy analysis to technocrat rational decision-making techniques does not challenge us to be critical of our goals and the purposes of policies. The danger lies in perpetuating the status quo and rewarding those who have always been included and continuing to exclude those who have been seen as unworthy or undeserving of help. We may revise our criteria, allocation methods and means, even redesign benefits, but as long as the values driving our goals are not directly debated, we risk unknowingly perpetuating existing goals and practices.

Policy analysis should not only provide a useful tool for determining the effectiveness and efficiency of public policies, it should be measured against the normative goals and values we seek to integrate in a society. Here, an alternative approach is offered, one that openly places a normative framework to sit prominently in analyses and to guide an ongoing process of reflection, choices, and understanding.

1.2   Rights-Based and Needs-Based Approaches to Social Policy Analysis

A rights-based approach guides social workers on how to integrate human rights principles into social work practice with the goal of developing long- and short-term responses to current social issues that further human rights. Human rights are integral to the enjoyment and safeguarding of human life, the achievement of human progress, the protection of human dignity, and the advancement of human security.

Most societies have long pursued a "basic needs" approach; that is, an approach based on identifying the basic requirements of human development and advocating within societies in favor of their fulfillment. Although human rights are need-based claims, a human rights approach differs from the basic needs approach in critical ways. A key difference is that the basic needs approach does not necessarily identify or imply responsibility for the need being met whereas in a human rights-based approach, a right is assigned to rights holders who claim their rights from duty bearers.

Rights entail obligations while needs do not. Duty bearers have a clear-cut duty to meet needs and if they do not, are violating the rights of rights holders. In a needs-based approach, needs are often satisfied through benevolent or charitable actions. Actions based on a human rights approach are based on *legal and moral obligations* to carry out a duty that will actualize one's right. In a needs-based approach, it is assumed that the person(s) with power/authority to allocate resources knows what is "needed" and how to best deliver that which has been deemed as necessary. This is quite different in a rights-based approach in which rights holders and duty bearers ideally contribute throughout the decision-making process and its implementation.

Rights holders or their representatives should participate in well-informed ways in the formulation, implementation, and monitoring of policies and programs and should be fully consulted in developing other state actions. This participatory process is empowering and contributes to rights holders' understanding of relevant issues and to their capacity for self-determination. In this way, rights-based approaches seek to transform societies by reallocating power and decision making. This is an outcome that is not inherent in needs-based approaches.

Another key difference in approaches is that the basic needs approach may or may not recognize patterns of historical marginalization whereas a rights-based approach aims to directly overcome marginalization by more equitable sharing of resources and power.

A needs-based approach typically establishes programmatic goals and the success of a policy intervention is often measured by the attainment of these goals. In a rights-based approach, the success of policy or program interventions is measured against the progressive realization of human rights. The decisions, actions, and conduct of political, economic, social, and institutional systems, and actors are evaluated by their contribution to the realization of rights. Rights-based social policy analysis also differs from needs-based approaches in that rights-based approach may focus on a particular set of rights but it recognizes that a range of rights will need to work in tandem in order for a right or set of rights to be realized. While there is no hierarchy of rights (indivisibility), some human rights are progressive while others are immediate. For example, the right to life, the right to equal expression before the law and freedom to express oneself—are immediate. Many of the social and economic rights however require the input of state resources and are implemented progressively based on available resources. States have the obligation to improve the realization of social, economic, and cultural rights such as working toward quality education for all children or the highest standard of health for all and at minimum to satisfy the essential level of each right. By nature then, rights-based approach calls for the measurement of outcomes over time not just at one point in time and recognizes the interrelatedness of multiple efforts (Table 1.1).

Table 1.1 Comparison of needs-based and rights-based approaches to social policy

	Needs-based approach	Rights-based approach
Assists individuals who are viewed:	As deserving of assistance and in need	As entitled to assistance
Action based on:	Charity or evidence of need	Legal and moral obligations Rights claims
Policy decisions are made by:	Experts and political elites	Wide participation of rights holders and duty bearers including beneficiaries, experts, and representatives
Monitors	Needs and outcomes	Process and outcomes Transformational changes
Evaluations	Measured against programmatic goals	Progressive realization of human rights with emphasis on those a policy seeks to affect including decisions and actions taken
Obligation to implement:	Is at the will of government	Is a legal requirement
Results are:	Used as deemed relevant by experts and policymakers	Required to be shared with rights holders and duty bearers
Policy goals are:	Stagnant and particular to specific policy	Provisional and subject to change as knowledge and understanding of rights evolve

The goal of rights-based approaches to policy analysis is for policies to facilitate a higher level of rights realization. Policy goals are provisional and subject to change because as we understand the fullness of issues and rights, our interpretations of rights realization changes and our practices need to be modified accordingly.

Traditional indicators need to be reconsidered because there is a different emphasis that a human rights-based approach brings to policies and programs. A rights-based approach measures monitor both the *process* and *outcome* of social work efforts; it relates *human rights principles*, including nondiscrimination, equality, participation, and accountability; and seeks to measure the *transformative change* between the *rights holders* and *duty bearers*.

Furthermore, up until recently, efforts to apply a rights-based approach to social policy analysis have been limited (Ife, 2008; Reichert, 2011; Wronka, 2008) and efforts by UN agencies have focused on standard setting, implementation, and monitoring. International agencies have devoted energies to the establishment of standards that have overemphasized western interpretations of human rights including civil and political rights. The overemphasis on civil and political rights has often narrowed human rights remit and restricted accurate diagnoses of human rights within states at the cost of emphasizing individual over collective rights, neglecting efforts to increase social inclusion and moderate inequalities. States have then been left to implement these international standards that may conflict with cultural, social, economic, and political contexts of countries, and may create defensive postures for states when monitored by international evaluators who tend to focus disproportionately on rights violations over rights-based solutions.

1.3 Social Policies and Human Rights

Although social security has played an integral role in many states for decades, it is in the last two decades that social policies and programs have been recognized for the role they play in stabilizing countries politically and economically—particularly in developing countries, and in supporting development. Increasingly, social policies and programs, often referred to as social protection systems, are viewed as an effective response to poverty and vulnerability in developing countries and as an essential component of economic and social development strategies (Devereux & Sabates-Wheeler, 2004). The last decade has seen a growing number of entities integrate a rights-based approach into their work and among United Nations (UN) agencies this has been long led by the International Labour Organization (ILO). A rights-based approach moves social protection from a policy option to an obligation for states and international governance structures (Van Ginneken, 2003). Article 22 of the Universal Declaration of Human Rights (UDHR) articulates the right to social security is a basic human right, "Everyone, as a member of society, has the right to social security and is entitled to realization, through national effort and international co-operation and in accordance with the organization and resources of each State, of the economic, social and cultural rights indispensable for his dignity and the free development of his personality." This right is echoed in Article 11 of the International Covenant on Economic, Social, and Cultural Rights and other major UN human rights documents.

Building on the recommendations of the United Nations Chief Executives Board on social protection floor initiatives beginning in 2009, a rights-based approach to social protection was furthered by obligating governments to ensure that all persons have the availability, continuity, geographical and financial access to essential services, such as water and sanitation, food and adequate nutrition, health, education, housing, and other social services such as asset saving information; and obligates states to provide a minimum income and livelihood security for poor and vulnerable populations such as children, people in active age groups with insufficient income, and older persons. By June 2012, 184 national delegations consisting of governments, workers, and employer representatives unanimously accepted ILO Recommendation No. 202 on social protection floors. Recommendation 202 is a short document with wide-ranging implications that progressively ensure higher levels of social security to as many people as possible. According to Recommendation 202, national social protection floors should include at least the following four social security guarantees:

- Access to a nationally defined set of goods and services, constituting essential health care, including maternity care, that meets the criteria of availability, accessibility, acceptability, and quality;
- Basic income security for children, at least at a nationally defined minimum level, providing access to nutrition, education, care, and any other necessary goods and services;
- Basic income security, at least at a nationally defined minimum level, for persons in active age who are unable to earn sufficient income, in particular in cases of sickness, unemployment, maternity, and disability; and

- Basic income security, at least at a nationally defined minimum level, for older persons.

Recommendation 202 declares 18 principles that should govern national social protection systems including rights-based principles of universality of protection, adequacy of protection, the obligation to define benefits by law, nondiscrimination, progressivity of implementation, acknowledging the diversity of methods and approaches, and the need for tripartite participation and public consultation on benefit levels and conditions, demanding respect for dignity of people covered, efficient complaints procedures, transparency, and financial, fiscal, and economic sustainability.

The implementation of social protection based on these principles should require all countries—developing and developed—to rethink the standards by which they judge their social policy outcomes.

In 2012 at Rio+20—the UN Conference on Sustainable Development—countries agreed to establish an intergovernmental process to develop a set of "*action-oriented, concise and easy to communicate*" sustainable development goals (SDGs) to help drive the implementation of sustainable development. The Rio+20 Conference produced a document, *The Future We Want*, articulating development agenda goals for the United Nations and its member countries beyond 2015. A 30-member Open Working Group (OWG) of the General Assembly was tasked with preparing a proposal on the SDGs. Unlike the MDGs, which allegedly were developed by a small, closed group of men, the United Nations has cast a wide net to include consultation from many groups on the content of the SDGs.

The General Assembly adopted the SDGs in the fall of 2015 to go into effect in 2016. These are 17 SDGs proposed by the Open Working Group.

1. End poverty in all its forms everywhere,
2. End hunger, achieve food security and improved nutrition, and promote sustainable agriculture,
3. Ensure healthy lives and promote well-being for all at all ages,
4. Ensure inclusive and equitable quality education and promote lifelong learning opportunities for all,
5. Achieve gender equality and empower all women and girls,
6. Ensure availability and sustainable management of water and sanitation for all,
7. Ensure access to affordable, reliable, sustainable, and modern energy for all,
8. Promote sustained, inclusive and sustainable economic growth, full and productive employment, and decent work for all,
9. Build resilient infrastructure, promote inclusive and sustainable industrialization, and foster innovation,
10. Reduce inequality within and among countries,
11. Make cities and human settlements inclusive, safe, resilient, and sustainable,
12. Ensure sustainable consumption and production patterns,
13. Take urgent action to combat climate change and its impacts,
14. Conserve and sustainably use the oceans, seas, and marine resources for sustainable development,

15. Protect, restore, and promote sustainable use of terrestrial ecosystems, sustainably manage forests, combat desertification and halt and reverse land degradation, and halt biodiversity loss,
16. Promote peaceful and inclusive societies for sustainable development, provide access to justice for all, and build effective, accountable, and inclusive institutions at all levels, and
17. Strengthen the means of implementation and revitalize the global partnership for sustainable development.

Within the goals are a proposed 169 targets that include reducing by at least half the number of people living in poverty by 2030, eradicating extreme poverty (people living on less than $1.25 a day), eliminating violence against women, and promoting the rule of law and equal access to justice.

The SDGs address some of the systemic barriers to sustainable development and also offer a more comprehensive and balanced understanding of the three dimensions of sustainable development—social, economic, and environmental—and the institutional/governance aspects. Whereas the MDGs focused exclusively on developing countries with limited attention to the dimensions of sustainability, the SDGs include all countries and place sustainability at the forefront.

While the SDGs have been criticized for being too many in number, lacking a "narrative of change" (Ostrom, 2014), not identifying the wide range of groups along with government needed to actualize the goals, and not articulating an ultimate goal, the SDGs reinforce the UN agencies move away from an exclusive needs-based justification. They move toward embracing a rights-based approach, as have key development nongovernmental organizations such as Oxfam, Save the Children, and World Vision in the last couple of decades (Gatenio Gabel, 2012). Yet, as UN human rights experts have observed, the SDGs should be anchored in international human rights standards to ensure that strong means for ensuring accountability are met (www.un.org/apps/news/story.asp?NewsID=49907Jan 26, 2015). The need for a stronger tie between human rights and social protection in particular was noted in the Special Rapporteur's report on human rights and social protection systems (Sepulveda & Nyst, 2012).

1.4 Rights-Based Approach to Social Policy Analysis

The rights-based approach offered here incorporates some of the steps of traditional social policy analyses but goes beyond this to analyze social policies from the perspective of how policies and programs effect or are expected to effect the realization of rights. The analysis should begin with a definition of the social issues/problem from a rights perspective including the use of international, regional, and country-specific laws and instruments that articulate rights to identify violations; and country-specific efforts and statements on policies and programs that have been designed to address or that impact the social issue/problem identified.

A rights-based approach does not prescribe specific social protection programs; rather, it evaluates policies and programs according to standards specified in human rights laws and instruments adopted by a country. The responsibility for implementation of social protection programs ultimately rests with the sovereign country. The framework presented here suggests that social policy and programs be analyzed according to cross-cutting human rights principles while keeping in mind the obligation states have regarding social, economic, and cultural rights to give priority to the most marginalized and vulnerable groups. According to UNRISD, a human rights-based approach has the following key attributes:

- The main objective of policies and programs should be to fulfill human rights.
- A human rights-based approach identifies rights holders and their entitlements and corresponding duty bearers and their obligations, and works toward strengthening the capacities of rights holders to make their claims and of duty bearers to meet their obligations.

Principles and standards derived from international human rights treaties should guide all policies and programming in all sectors and in all phases of the process (United Nations Research Institute for Social Development, 2015).

Drawing from the work for the UN Human Right's Council's Special Rapporteur (Sepulveda & Nyst, 2012), four cross-cutting human rights principle-based dimensions are identified as participation in the decision-making process, accountability, nondiscrimination, and equality. For each of these principles, relevant dimensions of these principles are suggested as the basis for analysis and examples of the types of indicators that may capture the realization of rights are suggested.

Because the analysis seeks to measure the progressive realization of rights, a baseline should be established from which negative, positive, and nonmovement can be measured. For example, have any human rights instruments been ratified since the baseline or have new laws incorporating the instruments been enacted? Have new facilities been built to increase access? Have local councils been established to increase citizen participation in policymaking? Depending on the type of social issue being examined, the dimensions and types of indicators used will be modified. Furthermore, new indicators of rights realization are called for which in some circumstances incorporate existing policy indicators.

1.4.1   Guidelines for a Rights-Based Approach to Social Policy Analysis

1. Identify the social issue/problem.

   (a) Identify the rights violated or compromised by the social issue using:
   - International and regional human rights laws and instruments.
   - National constitutions, laws, and regulations.
   - In-country policies addressing or affecting social issue.

   (b) Formulate the social issue/problem from a rights-based framework.

2. Contextualize the social issue/problem.

   (a) What is at the root of the social issue? How has society responded to the social issue historically?
   (b) Have there been unintended consequences of policy responses to the social issue? Describe them and how they have been addressed if at all?
   (c) Identify the stakeholders, rights holders, and duty bearers and their roles.
   (d) Who benefits from the policy as it exists? Who loses?
   (e) In what ways have policies affecting rights holders marginalized the population?
   (f) In what ways does the policy affect the realization of human rights beyond the scope of the policy? How do policies in other areas affect the realization of rights the current policy intends to address?

3. Analysis of dimension(s) according to cross-cutting human rights principles of participation, accountability, nondiscrimination, and equality (P.A.N.E.).

   (a) Participation.
       Social protection programs should strive to ensure that rights holders and duty bearers are both heard at every stage of the social protection process, from identifying the social issue through evaluation of the program. Special consideration should be given to giving voice to those who are historically marginalized due to ethnicity, gender, language, or ability and institutionalizing forums for expression so that power relations can be transformed by both the process of formulating policies and their implementation.
       • How do rights holders participate in the policymaking process? In what ways are the voices of rights holders not included in the policymaking process?

   (b) Accountability.
       As duty bearers, states hold the responsibility of implementing laws, policies, and programs that further the realization of human rights in the country. Information should be accessible and decision-making processes should be transparent. Policymakers, administrators, and others involved in policy formulation and allocation must be held accountable for their decisions and actions with clearly defined processes for persons to seek redress when they believe their rights have been violated regarding social protection.
       • Has the state enacted legislation, policies, and programs to address the social issue? Are these efforts on schedule? If not, why not?
       • Does state make information available and accessible in a timely manner on the progress of its efforts to address an identified social issue?
       • If citizens feel that they have unfairly been denied assistance, is the process to challenge the decision documented and without repercussions? Are accountability mechanisms in place with responsibility of implementation clear and open to input from all citizens?

(c) Nondiscrimination and equality.

These principles require the State to ensure that laws, policies, and practice relating to social protection are nondiscriminatory and that priority is given to protect the most vulnerable segments of the population. Social protection programs should be accessible to all persons including women, children, persons with disabilities and/or those living with HIV/AIDS, older persons, and ethnic minorities without stigmatizing beneficiaries and at all stages of the program (from design through the selection of beneficiaries).

• In what ways, if any, is the policy discriminatory? Socially unjust?
• Are benefits accessible, affordable, and adequate to all persons?

(d) Recommendations.

Develop policy recommendations to resolve the social issue/problem identified above that will further the realization of the human rights principles of P.A.N.E.

The following chapters further explore analyzing social protection policies from a rights-based approach. Chapter 2 explores reframing social issues from a rights-based perspective using the international and national instruments available. It helps readers move away from needs-based conceptualizations of social issues and human needs to rights-based approaches. The chapter reviews the basic human rights instruments and then illustrates how to apply the basic principles of participation, accountability, nondiscrimination, and transparency to social issues while considering the challenges that arise. In Chap. 3, the arduous task of finding human rights indicators is considered. Readers are introduced to a guide for choosing structural, process, and outcome indicators to analyze social policies. The application of the basic human rights principles of participation, accountability, nondiscrimination, and equity are applied to the selection of indicators. Possible data sources are shared. In the last chapter, the readers are asked to consider whether maternity and parental leaves should be considered a human right and why. The P.A.N.E. frame is used to analyze the maternity and parental leave policies in the United States.

1.5   Exercise: Is Health a Human Right?

Depending on the size of the group, it may be advantageous to break into smaller groups to discuss the following:

1. Defining the social issue as a right.

   In its Constitution, the World Health Organization defines health as the "a state of complete physical, mental and social well-being and not merely the absence of disease or infirmity." Adopted by the International Health Conference, New York, 19–22 June 1946.

Discuss the strengths and weaknesses of this definition. How would you define health? How do you think health is defined in the United States or other country?

What would it mean to have a right to "a state of complete physical, mental and social well-being and not merely the absence of disease or infirmity" in the United States or other country?

2. Locating a right in human rights law.

Every country in the world is now party to at least one human rights treaty addressing a health-related right, including the right to health and other rights related to conditions necessary for health. How is the right to health or rights related to conditions for health presented in the international laws, covenants, and conventions?

What legal documents address the right to health in the United States (or other country)? As defined in national law, what kinds of obligations does the right to health impose on the state? Has the right to health been realized in the United States (or other country)? Why or why not? What needs to be done?

3. The interdependence of rights.

According to the WHO, promoting and protecting health and respecting, protecting, and fulfilling human rights are inextricably linked (WHO, n.d.). Discuss the interdependence of health to other rights and how the stagnation or suppression of other rights can prevent the realization of the right to health.

- How might violations or lack of attention to human rights (such as harmful traditional practices, slavery, torture and inhuman and degrading treatment, violence against women) result in serious health consequences?
- Discuss how health policies and programs can promote or violate human rights in their design or implementation (e.g. freedom from discrimination, rights to participation, privacy, and information).
- In what ways could the vulnerability to ill health be reduced by taking steps to respect, protect, and fulfill human rights (e.g. freedom from discrimination on account of ethnicity, sex, and social status, and the rights to food and nutrition, water, education, and adequate housing)?

4. Exploring the complexity of rights and policies.

Read the following statements and discuss whether you agree or disagree with the statements and why.

- The right to health includes access to timely, acceptable, and affordable health care of appropriate quality. Yet, about 150 million people globally suffer financial catastrophe annually, and 100 million are pushed below the poverty line as a result of the escalating costs of health care. Regardless of the ability to pay, all people should have access to quality health care services.
- The right to health means that States must generate conditions in which everyone can be as healthy as possible. It does not mean the right to be healthy.
- Vulnerable and marginalized groups in societies tend to bear an undue proportion of health problems due to discrimination.

5. Analyzing a policy from rights-based principles.
   Analyze the progression of health policy in your country as a human right according to at least one of the cross-cutting human rights principles of P.A.N.E. Use the questions below to guide your analysis.

- Participation.
    - Who was involved in developing health care policy?
    - In what ways are the voices of rights holders included or not included in the policymaking process?
    - What mechanisms exist for citizens to express their opinion or modify health care policy? Are the methods influential? Why or why not?

- Accountability.
    - In what ways has the right to health been realized compared to 20 years ago?
    - Has government lived up to its promises regarding health care policy? Who monitors government's adherence to its policy goals? Is this done effectively? Is it widely published and accessible? Does the government self-evaluate its progress on health care policy?
    - If someone feels their right to health has been violated or denied, is there a process to challenge the decision? How is this done? Are there repercussions for the individual?

- Nondiscrimination and equality.
    - Does the health policy in the country apply to all or does it exclude certain groups? Was this intentional or unintended? What, if anything, is being to address the discrimination?
    - Who benefits from the policy as it exists? Who loses?
    - In what ways have policies affecting rights holders marginalized the population?
    - In what ways is health policy discriminatory, e.g. are benefits accessible, affordable, and adequate to all persons?

6. Recommendations.
   Develop policy recommendations to address the inadequacies of health policy identified above that will further the realization of the human rights.

References

Bardach, E. (1986). *The eight-step path of policy analysis (A handbook for practice)*. Berkley, CA: Berkeley Academic Press/Odin Readers.

Bardach, E. (2005). *A practical guide for policy analysis* (2nd ed.). Washington, DC: CQ Press.

Blank, R. (2002). Evaluating welfare reform in the United States, Working Paper 8983. Cambridge, MA: National Bureau of Economic Research. Retrieved October 29, 2014, from http://www.nber.org/papers/w8983.

Bollen, K. A., & Bollen, P. (2000). Subjective measures of liberal democracy. *Comparative Political Studies, 33*, 58–86.

Chambers, D. E. (2000). The analysis of policy goals and objectives in social programs and policies. In D. E. Chambers (Ed.), *Social policy and social programs: A method for the practical public policy analyst* (pp. 79–109). Boston: Allyn & Bacon.

DeLeon, P. (1997). *Democracy and the policy sciences.* Albany, NY: SUNY Press.

Devereux, S., & Sabates-Wheeler, R. (2004). *Transformative social protection,* IDS Working Paper 232, IDS.

DiNitto, D. M. (1995). *Social welfare: Politics and public policy.* Boston: Allyn & Bacon.

Dobelstein, A. W. (1996). *Social welfare: Policy and analysis.* Lanham, MD: Rowman & Littlefield Publishers.

Fischer, F. (2003). *Reframing public policy: Discursive politics and deliberative practices: Discursive politics and deliberative practices.* Oxford: Oxford University Press.

Gatenio Gabel, S. (2012). Social protection and children in developing countries. *Children and Youth Services Review, 34*(537), 545.

Gilbert, N., & Terrell, P. (1986). *Dimensions of social welfare policy* (2nd ed.). Englewood Cliffs, NJ: Prentice-Hall.

Gilbert, N., & Terrell, P. (2005). *Dimensions of social welfare policy* (6th ed.). Boston, MA: Pearson Education, Inc.

Ife, J. (2008). *Human rights and social work,* Revised edition. Cambridge, UK: Cambridge University Press.

Ingram, H., & Smith, S. (1998). Institutions and policies for democracy: A discussion paper and comments. *Policy Currents, 8,* 1–13.

Lasswell, H. D. (1971). *A pre-view of policy sciences.* New York: American Elsevier Publishing Co.

Lasswell, H. D., & Lerner, D. (Eds.). (1951). *The policy sciences.* Palo Alto, CA: Stanford University Press.

Martin, J., Hamilton, B. E., Osterman, J. K., Curtain, S., & Mathews, T. J. (2015). Births: Final data for 2013. *National Vital Statistics Reports, 64*(1), 1–65.

Moran, M., Goodin, R.E. & Rein, M. (2006). Introduction: The public and its policies. In R. E. Goodin, M. Rein, & M. Moran, (Eds.) The Oxford handbook of public policy. p. 5.

Myrdal, A. (1968). *Nation and family: The Swedish experiment in democratic family and population policy.* Cambridge: MIT Press.

Nelson, R. (1977). *The moon and the ghetto.* New York, NY: W.W. Norton & Company.

Ostrom, E. (2014). J collective action and the evolution of social norms. *Journal of Natural Resources Policy Research, 6*(4), 235–252.

Reichert, E. (2011). *Social work and human rights: A foundation for policy and practice* (2nd ed.). New York, NY: Columbia University Press.

Sepulveda, M., & Nyst, C. (2012). *The human rights approach to social protection.* Enwiko Oy, Finland: Ministry for foreign Affairs of Finland.

Smith, K. B., & Larimer, C. W. (2009). *The public policy theory primer* (pp. 1–26). Boulder, CO: Westview Press.

Sodaro, M. J. (2004). *Comparative politics. A global introduction.* New York: McGraw Hill.

Stone, D. (2002). *Policy paradox: The art of political decision making.* New York, NY: W.W. Norton & Company.

Stone, D. (2011). *The policy paradox: The art of decision making,* Revised Edition. New York, NY: W.W. Norton & Company.

United Nations Research Institute for Social Development (UNRISD). (2015). Framework for a human rights-based approach to social protection. UNRISD. Retrieved July 2015, from www.unrisd.org/unrisd/.../2461D8D13FF94049C1257D420031B997.

Van Ginneken, W. (2003). Extending social security: Policies for developing countries. *International Labour Review, 142,* 277–294.

Wronka, J. (2008). *Human rights and social justice: Social action and service for the helping and health professions.* Thousand Oaks, CA: Sage.

Chapter 2
Understanding Human Rights and Social Policy

In the United States, the earliest identification of AIDS as a gay disease, a "gay cancer," or a "gay plague" continued to dominate public perception and shape official responses long after the name "acquired immune deficiency syndrome" was adopted to replace the term "gay-related immunodeficiency disease." Despite mounting evidence of heterosexual transmission, some religious leaders seized on the chance to identify HIV/AIDS with the gay community, arguing that the disease was God's punishment for sin and that homosexuals should be tattooed or quarantined. In September 1985, 4 years after the disease appeared, President Reagan mentioned AIDS publicly for the first time at a press conference, adding to the confusion by implying that casual contact could transmit HIV. When asked if he would send his own children to school with a child who had AIDS, Reagan commented that although the medical evidence suggested this would not put them at risk, there was no unequivocal proof.

The combination of denial and panic that characterized the response in the United States was echoed around the world. Many African countries refused to pay attention to HIV/AIDS and deeply resented the fact that Western scientists viewed Africa as the origin of the disease. Chinese officials argued that as there were no homosexuals, drug users, or prostitutes within the People's Republic, there was, therefore, no AIDS. In Germany, a federal judge declared that it might be necessary to tattoo and quarantine people carrying the virus. In the first decade of AIDS, 104 countries adopted restrictive AIDS-related laws. When the development of a test for HIV made it possible to identify carriers of the disease, such legislation soared. The epidemic also spawned a particular type of hate crime, in which those thought to be at high risk of contracting the disease and people living with AIDS were verbally and physically assaulted.

Elizabeth Fee & Manon Parry, 2008.

During the first few years of the appearance of the AIDS epidemic, the disease was publicly identified as belonging to US gay men and soon later to intravenous drug users. Responses to the disease were to marginalize and isolate those infected, deny the existence of the epidemic, and finger point. It is unlikely that the significant advances we have made in combating the spread and treatment of HIV/AIDS would have occurred if we had clung to the early perspectives of the disease that called for isolation and alienation of persons with HIV/AIDS. Early editions of the UNAIDS *Global report on the AIDS epidemic* were filled with

© Springer International Publishing Switzerland 2016
S. Gatenio Gabel, *A Rights-Based Approach to Social Policy Analysis*,
SpringerBriefs in Rights-Based Approaches to Social Work,
DOI 10.1007/978-3-319-24412-9_2

gloom and doom and have since given way to more promise, including historic declines in AIDS-related deaths and new HIV infections as well as unprecedented preventive and maintenance efforts in HIV-related activities in low- and middle-income countries (UNAIDS, 2013). By placing AIDS/HIV in the context of other social issues, our understanding of the factors related to vulnerability expanded and we were able to halt and more recently reverse the AIDS epidemic. We now share a global vision of zero new infections and AIDS-related deaths where people living with HIV/AIDS no longer experience discrimination (UNAIDS, 2013). The reframing of AIDS from its early days as a population-specific disease is largely due to the relentless efforts of the late Jonathan Mann.

Jonathan Mann was the first director of the Global AIDS Program at the World Health Organization (WHO) from 1986 to 1990. Mann helped the world understand that the biological and behavioral origins of AIDS were only part of the story and to fully address the disease and halt its spread, we had to understand how sociopolitical, economic, and cultural factors contributed to the disease. This went against conventional thinking at the time that rarely linked disease eradication with socioeconomic and political factors.

One of the first actions Mann took was to challenge the quarantine and exclusion of persons living with HIV/AIDS (PLWHA). By 1987, more than 80 % of countries had laws to control PLWHAs or people thought to be at risk of infection, such as the men who have sex with men and sex workers, and discrimination in housing, travel, health care, and employment was common (Patterson, 2009). Mann believed that discrimination would only drive the infected underground, making it harder to track the epidemic and treat people with the disease (Fee & Parry, 2008). Recognizing that social exclusion added vulnerability to HIV infection, Mann stressed that the violation of rights due to a person's race, gender, sexual orientation, education level, nationality, and/or income concurred with the political repression, unemployment, migration, cultural practices that devalue persons and limit their opportunities to live their lives to the fullest potential (Patterson, 2009). He saw information on prevention as an important component of limiting the spread of the disease.

Working with other activists and scholars in the 1990s, Mann framed HIV/AIDS from a rights-based approach arguing that health is a human right. As a human right, he noted the interdependence of health on other human rights (civil, socioeconomic, and cultural) and the basic principles underlying all human rights—inalienability, universal, indivisibility, interdependence, and nondiscrimination (Mann et al., 1999). He based his argument on the International Bill of Human Rights that has been signed by two-thirds of UN country members. The International Bill of Rights includes three documents: the UDHR, the International Covenant on Economic, Social and Cultural Rights (ICESCR), and the International Covenant on Political and Civil Rights (ICPCR). Article 25 of the UDHR declares: "Everyone has the right to a standard of living adequate for the health and well-being of himself and of his family, including food, clothing, housing and medical care and necessary social services, and the right to security in … sickness disability … old age…" Article 12 of the ICESCR states: "the right of everyone to the enjoyment of the highest attainable standard of physical and mental health" and identifies some of the measures the state should take "to achieve the full realization of this right."

The ICCPR refers to political and civil rights affecting public health and Article 26 of the ICCPR makes clear that "All persons are equal before the law and are entitled without any discrimination to the equal protection of the law" thus reinforcing that all health services, goods, and facilities must be provided to all without any discrimination. The right of persons to participate in public affairs and to equal access to public services is articulated in Article 25 of the ICPCR. Fusing civil and political rights with socioeconomic rights is a critical component of a rights-based approach. As noted by Stainton (2005), the key elements in shifting to a rights-based approach is in providing opportunities for people to articulate their claims; to identify, obtain, and manage supports necessary to actualize their claims; to have control over resources and in governance; or for decision making within relevant structures.

Using a rights-based frame, the causes of AIDS/HIV were understood to have biological, behavioral, social, political, and economic roots, and societal responses shifted from marginalization to enforceable, legal entitlements. By situating AIDS within a human rights frame, Mann was able to expose inequities in health systems across societies and the relationship between social inequalities and the presence of HIV/AIDS both within countries and across countries (Fee & Parry, 2008). Indeed, Mann and his colleagues were able to demonstrate the two-directional interdependence of human rights and health/well-being (Mann et al., 1999). Countries have the responsibility to work with citizens toward the realization of rights (making rights an entitlement) and are accountable to its citizens and global partners. Framing PLWHA as rights holders also reinforced their right to participate in AIDS policymaking. Looking at the success in the United States of the Gay Men's Health Crisis (GMHC) and the AIDS Coalition to Unleash Power (ACTUP) who used education about HIV prevention, captured media attention on AIDS, and the active involvement of PLWHA in influencing government policies, Mann incorporated these strategies into WHO global partnerships with bilateral donors, governments, and civil societies.

Shifting to a conceptualization of social issues from a rights-based frame can be daunting because we have a tendency to entrench ourselves in a particular perspective so deeply that we can easily and unknowingly come to see our perspective as unbiased even when it is colored by cultural norms and prejudices. By recasting social issues from a rights-based perspective, we go beyond cultural norms and embrace global normative standards. A rights-based approach often involves wide-ranging and synergistic efforts of diverse stakeholders including governments, solidarity among the international community, civil society, and scientific innovation because the roots of social issues are interdependent and expose the inequities within societies.

The purpose of this chapter is to help the reader reframe social issues from a rights-based perspective using the international and national instruments available. It helps readers move away from needs-based and charity-based conceptualizations of social issues and human needs to rights-based approaches. The chapter begins by reviewing the basic human rights instruments and then illustrates how to apply the basic principles of participation, accountability, nondiscrimination, and transparency to social issues. A discussion of the challenges that arise follows as well as the types of analyses that may be used.

2.1   International Human Rights Instruments

Familiarity with the international human rights instruments is essential to practice and may be one of the reasons the legal profession often leads to rights-based efforts. To practice from a rights-based approach, a practitioner must be familiar with the major international, regional, and domestic instruments that articulate modern human rights. It is also important to understand how these instruments evolved and why laws are structured differently across countries. A summary of the major instruments and mechanisms is offered below.

Modern human rights arose in response to the atrocities committed during World War II. The inhumanity exhibited made clear that protections existing at the time were inadequate to safeguard individuals and their rights from government violations. The Universal Declaration of Human Rights (UDHR), which is nonbinding, was unanimously accepted by the United Nations General Assembly on December 10, 1948. In the years to follow, the countries at the United Nations set out to create binding human rights treaties that defined the rights of humans with the force of law and with more specificity than the UDHR offered.

Declaration is a document stating standards or principles, but which is not legally binding
Treaty, convention, covenant, charter is legally binding agreement between two or more countries
Ratification is a formal process by which a country agrees to be bound by the terms of a treaty
Reservation is the exception that States make to a treaty (e.g., provisions within the treaty the government does not accept)

The human rights treaty process is usually initiated by legal and subject matter experts who participate in crafting a draft of a treaty at the United Nations. Representatives of interested countries will then negotiate the final terms or content of the treaty. The process can become lengthy if many countries join the drafting process and there are conflicting perspectives. The time it takes to develop an international human rights standard expressed in treaty form can vary widely. For example, it took less than 2 years for the UDHR to be written and 18 years for the United Nations to produce the covenants that spell out our political,

Table 2.1 Human rights in the International Bill of Rights

The International Bill of Rights
Universal Declaration of Human Rights
International Covenant on Civil and Political Rights
International Covenant on Social, Economic, and Cultural Rights

- The right to equality and freedom from discrimination
- The right to life, liberty, and personal security
- Freedom from torture and degrading treatment
- The right to equality before the law
- The right to a fair trial
- The right to privacy
- Freedom of belief and religion
- Freedom of opinion
- Right of peaceful assembly and association
- The right to participate in government
- The right to self-determination
- The right to social security
- The right to work
- The right to form trade unions and work under favorable conditions
- The right to an adequate standard of living
- The right to education
- The right to health
- The right to food and housing
- The right to take part in cultural life
- The right to benefit from scientific progress

civil, economic, social, and cultural rights. Recommendations may be offered from nongovernmental organizations during the process.

Once the final version is agreed upon, the treaty is opened for country ratification. Countries have different methods for acceding to or ratifying treaties. In the United States, the President first signs a treaty and then two-thirds of the US Senate must vote in favor of the treaty for it to be ratified. By ratifying a treaty, a country agrees to be legally bound by the terms of the treaty. Countries that ratify may object to certain parts of the treaty and express this by entering reservations to their ratification. In this way, a country agrees to uphold the treaty with noted exceptions or limitations. A country may enter a reservation because it conflicts with certain provisions or it is inconsistent with a country's own constitution. Once a country ratifies a covenant, convention, or treaty, a country has responsibility to integrate and implement it into its own constitution and laws (Table 2.1).

The most significant components of the human rights statutory framework are the two covenants adopted as legal treaties in 1966: the International Covenant on Civil and Political Rights and the International Covenant on Economic, Social and Cultural Rights. Although originally envisioned as a single, unified Covenant on Human Rights, a decision was taken in the back rooms of the UN to produce two separate standards, a "Political Covenant" and an "Economic Covenant." Why two treaties when the purpose was to forge ahead in a unified vision? The explanation often given is that while political and civil rights detailed in the ICCPR require immediate implementation, the implementation of social and economic rights is gradual or progressive and countries needed the time to establish systems for guaranteeing social and economic rights. However, this appears to be more of a post-facto justification, and most believe the decision to split the covenants was ideologically motivated.

The division of rights between the two covenants is artificial, reflecting the global ideological divide of the period. This was the time of the Cold War, colonialism was being dismantled and a new polarized division of power was being created that required allegiance to either the East or to the West. The two covenants came to represent the competing visions of the two super powers—the United States and its allies championing the individual rights manifest in the ICCPR; the Soviet Union and its allies championing the collective rights of the ICESCR. This split between political and civil from social and economic rights undermined the very core of a shared vision for human rights. It also subverted the integration of the principles of indivisibility and interdependence of human rights by establishing fundamentally different approaches to understanding and implementing the two sets of rights and simultaneously closed off international scrutiny and accountability. It was only after the collapse of the Soviet Union that a greater effort was made to integrate civil and political rights with economic, social, and cultural rights.

In many ways, the United States led the West in its pursuit of political and civil rights. The US Bill of Rights is often cited as one of the first public documents of modern human rights, Eleanor Roosevelt chaired the committee who wrote the UDHR, and the United States has committed billions of dollars in aid to expose and root out human rights abuses throughout the world. However, the United States has had an ambivalent relationship with international human rights law and has only ratified three of the major international human rights treaties: the ICCPR, the Convention against Torture (CAT), and the Convention on the Elimination of All Forms of Racial Discrimination (CERD). And the United States is one of only a handful of countries that has not ratified important treaties like the Convention on the Elimination of All Forms of Discrimination against Women (CEDAW) and is the only country not to ratify the Convention on the Rights of the Child (CRC). Nor has the United States signed regional documents upholding human rights in the Americas (Table 2.2).

This notable lack of ratification is known as U.S. exceptionalism in human rights policy. On the one hand, the United States has initiated and arguably demanded the compliance of human rights abroad—while on the other hand, it has repeatedly rejected the application of international standards for human rights in the United States. By refusing to ratify the interdependent multilateral human rights norms, the United States stands nearly alone among western democracies failing to offer its citizens the opportunities to seek remedies for internationally codified rights before either a domestic or international tribunal. Critics have noted the double-standard perpetuated by the United States who holds other

Table 2.2   Status of major human rights treaties in the United States

	UN Adoption	US Signature	US Ratification
International Convention on the Elimination of All Forms of Racial Discrimination	1965	4 Jan 1969	20 Nov 1994
International Covenant on Economic, Social and Cultural Rights	1966	5 Oct 1977	Not ratified
International Covenant on Civil and Political Rights	1966	5 Oct 1977	8 Jun 1992
Convention on the Elimination of All Forms of Discrimination against Women	1979	17 Jul 1980	Not ratified
Convention against Torture and Other Cruel, Inhuman, or Degrading Treatment or Punishment	1984	18 Apr 1988	21 Oct 1994
Convention on the Rights of the Child	1989	16 Feb 1995	Not ratified
Convention on the Protection of the Rights of All Migrant Workers and Members of Their Families	1990	Not signed	Not ratified
Convention on the Rights of Persons with Disabilities	2006	2009	Not ratified
Convention for the Protection of All Persons from Enforced Disappearance	2006	Not signed	Not ratified

nations accountable to these international standards and laws while exempting itself (Hertel & Libal, 2011).

Although the ICCPR and ICESCR keep civil and political separate from socio-economic and cultural rights, subsequent human rights treaties adopted by the United Nations to address the situation of especially vulnerable populations reintegrated these different types of rights and created normative standards on rights as well as legal obligations on states to respect, protect, and implement human rights in their countries.

2.1.1   Duty Bearers

Governments have the primary responsibility for protecting and promoting human rights but businesses, civil society, and individuals are also responsible for ensuring human rights. According to the Preamble of the UDHR, "Every individual and every organ of society … shall strive by teaching and education to promote respect for these rights and freedoms and by progressive measures, national and international, to secure their universal and effective recognition and observance."

When a government ratifies a human rights treaty, it assumes a legal obligation to respect, protect, and fulfill the rights contained in the treaty (see Table 2.3). Governments are obligated to both prevent human rights violations against people within their territories and to provide effective remedies for those whose rights are violated.

Table 2.3 Human rights and the roles of government

Respect	Protect	Fulfill
Governments must not act in ways that deprive people of a right or interfere with persons exercising their rights	*Governments must prevent private actors from violating the human rights of others*	*Governments and other responsible parties must take positive action to facilitate the enjoyment of basic human rights through the establishment of political, economic, and social systems*
For example, governments: • Can create constitutional guarantees of human rights • Cannot deprive certain communities or populations access to health care facilities or schools • Should not allow the abuse or a discrimination against persons with disabilities, children, women, or any other persons • Should ratify international human rights treaties	For example, governments: • Can enact and enforce laws prohibiting private companies from releasing hazardous chemicals that impair public health • Should prosecute perpetrators of human rights abuses, such as crimes of child abuse and neglect or discrimination against persons with disabilities • Can educate people about human rights and the importance of respecting the human rights of others	For example, governments: • Should provide free, high-quality public education • Can create a public defender system so that everyone has access to a lawyer • May ensure everyone has access to clean water and food by funding public assistance programs • Can launch a public education campaign on the right to vote

2.1.2 Regional Human Rights Instruments

In addition to international human rights instruments, there are three regional human rights mechanisms in force in Africa, the Americas, and Europe. Regional mechanisms (i.e., treaties, declarations, commissions, and courts) complement the UN human rights system and do not detract from the obligations that states have already undertaken by ratifying the core international human rights treaties. Regional mechanisms help countries realize human rights by promoting human rights regionally that in turn provide incentives for governments to engage in the promotion of human rights within their own territories; establishing regional mechanisms such as courts or treaties that may provide more culturally accepted and sensitive interpretations of human rights; and by helping implementation efforts in countries through regional commissions, special rapporteurs, and courts (Petersen, 2011). Regional mechanisms can also facilitate regional input to the development of international human rights standards and mechanisms and can help national governments address regional human rights concerns that cross national borders—for example, human rights concerns related to migration, transnational crime, and environmental disasters.

Currently, well-established regional human rights systems exist in Africa, the Americas, and Europe. The regional arrangements for protecting human rights in

Europe are extensive, involving the Council of Europe, the European Union, and the Organization for Security and Cooperation in Europe. Some of the most long-standing and developed of intergovernmental instruments are housed in the Council of Europe, and include the 1950 Convention for the Protection of Human Rights and Fundamental Freedoms and the European Social Charter, and intergovernmental mechanisms include the European Court of Human Rights and the European Committee for the Prevention of Torture and Inhuman or Degrading Treatment or Punishment (Petersen, 2011).

In the Americas, regional human rights are the primary responsibility of the Organisation of American States. The main human rights instruments in the inter-American system are the 1948 American Declaration on the Rights and Duties of Man and the legally binding American Convention on Human Rights. The main mechanisms include the Inter-American Commission on Human Rights and the Inter-American Court of Human Rights.

Created by the African Union, the main regional human rights instrument in Africa is the 1981 African Charter on Human and Peoples' Rights, and the main mechanisms are the African Commission on Human and Peoples' Rights and the recently established African Court on Human and Peoples' Rights, to be merged with the African Court of Justice.

A regional mechanism does not currently exist for Asia.

Each of the regional mechanisms are subordinate to national human rights mechanisms but can issue binding decisions and reparations regarding human rights violations.

Rights must be protected by domestic legal systems according to the preamble of the UDHR, "it is essential, if man is not to be compelled to have recourse, as a last resort, to rebellion against tyranny and oppression, that human rights should be protected by the rule of law." By signing an international treaty, States are obligated to incorporate expressed rights into their constitutions and domestic laws, and are responsible for violations of their treaty obligations even when not intentional.

Policy analysis undertaken from a rights-based approach should therefore situate the social issue by reviewing which international and regional treaties a country has ratified and assess the incorporation of the treaty or treaties into domestic law at all relevant levels of governance.

In addition to these legal provisions, comments and resolutions by UN bodies should be considered when conducting a policy analysis from a rights-based approach because they may contribute to international custom and in certain circumstances be regarded as having legal value (OHCHR, 2012). An example of this is the UDHR, which is not legally binding but is considered evidence of customary international law. Customary international law refers to international obligations arising from established state practice, as opposed to obligations arising from formal written international treaties. Customary international law results from a general and consistent practice of states that they follow from a sense of legal obligation (Shaw, 2003).

The broad range of human rights instruments presents a challenge to ensure the application of the law to specific areas and to effectively coordinate the different

Table 2.4 Human rights treaty bodies

Human Rights Committee (CCPR) monitors implementation of the International Covenant on Civil and Political Rights (1966) and its optional protocols
Committee on Economic, Social and Cultural Rights (CESCR) monitors implementation of the International Covenant on Economic, Social and Cultural Rights (1966)
Committee on the Elimination of Racial Discrimination (CERD) monitors implementation of the International Convention on the Elimination of All Forms of Racial Discrimination (1965)
Committee on the Elimination of Discrimination against Women (CEDAW) monitors implementation of the Convention on the Elimination of All Forms of Discrimination against Women (1979) and its optional protocol (1999)
Committee against Torture (CAT) monitors implementation of the Convention against Torture and Other Cruel, Inhuman, or Degrading Treatment (1984)
Committee on the Rights of the Child (CRC) monitors implementation of the Convention on the Rights of the Child (1989) and its optional protocols (2000)
Committee on Migrant Workers (CMW) monitors implementation of the International Convention on the Protection of the Rights of All Migrant Workers and Members of Their Families (1990)
Committee on the Rights of Persons with Disabilities (CRPD) monitors implementation of the International Convention on the Rights of Persons with Disabilities (2006)
Committee on Enforced Disappearances (CED) monitors implementation of the International Convention for the Protection of All Persons from Enforced Disappearance (2006)

elements within an expanding system. Ten treaty committees were created to monitor the implementation of the nine core international human rights treaties. Each committee is composed of independent experts of recognized competence in human rights, who are nominated and elected for fixed renewable terms of 4 years by State parties. The treaty bodies meet in Geneva, Switzerland.

Each of the treaty bodies publishes its interpretation of the provisions of its respective human rights treaty in the form of "general comments" or "general recommendations." These cover a wide range of subjects from the comprehensive interpretation of substantive provisions to general guidance on the information that should be submitted in State reports relating to specific articles of the treaties.

General comments have also dealt with wider, cross-cutting issues such as the role of national human rights institutions, the rights of persons with disabilities, violence against women, and the rights of minorities. Sometimes, issues arise that were not considered when the treaties were first written. For example, CEDAW, as adopted in 1979, specifically addresses discrimination against women yet omitted any provisions on violence against women. Two general recommendations were published by the CEDAW Committee in 1989 and 1992, Nos. 12 and 19, respectively, violence against women as a form of discrimination against women is explicitly cited (CEDAW Committee, 1989, 1992). In No. 19, the CEDAW Committee defined discrimination to include "gender-based violence, that is violence that is directed against a woman because she is a woman or that affects woman disproportionately … physical, mental or sexual harm or suffering, threat of such acts, coercion or other deprivations of liberty" (para. 6). Likewise, while the ICESCR delineates the responsibility of state parties not to discriminate on the basis of race, color, sex, language, political or other opinion, national or social origin, property, birth or other status, it is silent on discrimination on the basis of sexual preference or identification. It is in General Comment No. 20 of the UN Committee for Economic, Social and Cultural Rights that offers the term "other status" in the ICESCR to include "sexual orientation" and "gender identity," thereby making them protected classes like race, religion, origin, and birth status. Not everyone agrees with this interpretation or that a Committee should have the right to reinterpret a treaty after it has been signed. For example, the African Group requested that sexual orientation and gender identity references to General Comments 19 and 20 issued by the Economic, Social and Cultural Rights Committee be deleted (Family Watch International, 2009).

Additionally, the United Nations General Assembly may pass resolutions affecting human rights that are generally nonbinding but can explain intention or provide guidance to members.

2.2   Grounding Social Policies in Legal and Institutional Frameworks

A rights-based approach to social policies should be solidly based in legal and institutional instruments within a country to insure policy stability and the recognition of beneficiaries as rights holders. Policies that are integrated into national action plans and other long- and short-term social policy strategies increase the likelihood that social protection will become available for all, and especially for the most disadvantaged and vulnerable groups. It also helps ensure that social protection measures are guarded from political manipulation and that they receive lasting commitment from state authorities, regardless of change of government leaders. According to the UNRISD, an adequate legal framework is one that includes:

- Detailed eligibility requirements for social protection programs;
- Mechanisms to ensure transparency and access to information about available programs;
- Defines the various roles and responsibilities of all those involved in implementing the programs at different levels of government;
- Identifies a clear institutional framework to enable rights holders to identify duty bearers in charge of specific responsibilities;
- Articulates long-term financial requirements, ensuring adequacy and predictability of benefits;
- Makes complaints and appeal mechanisms available and accessible; and
- Participation channels for all beneficiaries.

General Comment 19 of the UN Committee on Economic, Social and Cultural Rights (2008) provides further discussion on the expectation of social policies and programs and human rights standards.

In addition to understanding the legal framework for a policy, it is also important to ground a particular policy, its programs, benefits, and services within the overall social protection scheme of a country. Social protection schemes are generally considered to have four basic components: social insurance (usually funded by contributions from formal sector employees toward support against risks such as health, old age, disability, unemployment), social assistance (noncontributory support for poor and marginalized sometimes referred to as social safety nets), social supports (services to support disadvantaged, vulnerable, and marginalized groups or services), and social justice (laws, regulations, justice systems to address sociopolitical conditions creating vulnerability and marginalization). This categorization reflects the comprehensiveness, diversity, and purpose of social protection efforts but falls short of helping us understand how social protection efforts may introduce or impede social change and the realization of rights.

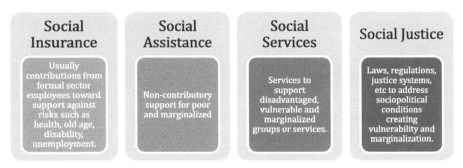

It may be useful to reframe social policies with regard to their primary purpose and how they contribute to the realization of rights. Devereux and Sabates-Wheeler (2004) offer an example of rights-based framework to assess the ability of social protection efforts to socially transform a society by offering opportunities for socially vulnerable groups to participate in individual and economic growth. To be comprehensive, the cumulative efforts should offer all four components of the framework and as such it may be useful for an analysis to consider not only the policy or program but also how it fits in to the overarching scheme (Gatenio Gabel, 2014). The four main elements of this framework are:

- *Provision measures* to provide relief from deprivation, such as narrowly targeted safety nets for people facing livelihood shocks (e.g., food aid as emergency relief) and social assistance for the chronically poor (e.g., disability benefit, social pensions).
- *Preventive measures* to avert deprivation, including formal social insurance schemes (e.g., health insurance, unemployment benefits), informal risk-pooling mechanisms (e.g., savings clubs, burial societies), and diversification strategies to spread risk.
- *Promotive measures* to enhance incomes and capabilities in the short- and long-term (e.g., school feeding or public works with skill training).

• *Transformative measures* to address vulnerabilities arising from social inequity and exclusion (e.g., protecting minority ethnic groups against discrimination or sensitization campaigns on HIV and AIDS). Transformative measures address the power imbalances in society that create and sustain vulnerabilities within population groups and within households.

2.3 Conceptualizing Social Issues from a Human Rights Frame

The interrelatedness of human rights is key to conceptualizing social issues from a human rights framework. Rarely, in rights-based approaches can one right violation be isolated. Likewise, when we conceptualize developing social policies to promote the realization of rights, we can focus social protection efforts on the promotion of certain rights but need to be cognizant that efforts will likely affect a full array of rights. Rights-based efforts should not only consider the effects programs or policies may have on other social or economic rights, but should also consider the effects of policies or programs on political and civil rights. Our conventional needs- and charity-based methods typically neglect political and civil rights when analyzing social policies and programs.

The example of child marriage is used here to illustrate how a social issue is reframed from a rights-based approach. Child marriage occurs when at least one or both partners in a marriage is under the age of 18 years (this definition of child is used by the Convention on the Rights of the Child). Both girls and boys may be affected by child marriage, but the majority of child marriages occur between a girl who is under 18 years old and a male who is over 18 years of age. One-third of the world's girls are married before the age of 18 and one in nine are married before the age of 15 (ICRW, 2007). Research findings indicate that the consequences of girls marrying before they are the age of majority can be severe (United Nations Population Fund, 2012). Girls who marry before age 18 are more likely to experience abuse, violence, and exploitation than those who marry as adults. Bearing and delivering children prematurely may impair reproductive organs and the health of the young mother and her child(ren). An example of this is obstetric fistula, a condition that leaves two million females leaking urine or feces due to prolonged labor and injury to the birth canal and is especially common among physically immature girls (United Nations Children's Fund, 2009). Approximately 15 million females between the ages of 15 and 19 years give birth each year and girls under the age of 15 are five times more likely to die during pregnancy or childbirth than women in their twenties (United Nations Children's Fund, 2009). Children born to adolescent mothers are 60 % more likely to die than infants born to mothers over 19 years (United Nations Children's Fund, 2009). Girls who marry young typically leave school and are subject to isolation from family and friends leaving them unprepared for the psychosocial and emotional consequences they are forced to confront.

Young girl brides are more likely to be abused and be victims of domestic violence than women who marry when they are older (IPPF & FMRWG, 2006). For young brides, leaving an abusive home is often not seen as an option because of economic pressures and cultural expectations. Young brides who have left their marriage have been reported to suffer from social and economic stigma, punished or killed by close male kin for bringing shame upon the family, or left to fend for themselves with little legal recourse (IPPF, 2006).

Unlike traditional policy analyses that might frame child marriage as a social problem because it removes girls from school or that initiates a pattern of dependency, a rights-based approach first looks to international and national human rights instruments to frame this social issue. In this case, Article 16 of the UDHR states that all persons "of full age" have a right to "free and full consent" to a marriage implying that partners who are not fully mature may not be in a position to make a fully cognizant decision. Typically, the fathers of the bride and groom or an elder in the family arrange child marriages. CEDAW specifies in Article 16 that "the betrothal and marriage of a child shall have no legal effect and all necessary action, including legislation, shall be taken to specify a minimum age of marriage." The CEDAW Committee General Recommendation 21 determines that 18 should be the minimum age for marriage for men and women.

Interestingly, the CRC does not explicitly address marriage although child marriage may be a violation of children's other rights articulated in the CRC such as Articles 12 and 13 (the right to express one's views), Articles 19, 34, 35, and 36 (the right to be protected from exploitation and abuse) and Article 24 (the right to be protected from harmful practices). Child marriage often curtails a child's education and relocates girls to live in isolating and/or abusive situations that may violate related rights such as the right to education, information, to rest and leisure, to health, to protection against physical and mental violence and abuse, and from being separated from their parents against the child's or parent's will (see the CRC Articles 9, 17, 19, 20, 24, 28, 28, 29, 30, 31, and 32). The CRC General Comment 4 notes that all states are obligated to protect adolescents from all harmful traditional practices that are harmful to children's health. The next step would be to consider if there were regional human rights instruments that address the social issue. For example, the African Charter on the Rights and Welfare of the Child (1990) prohibits marriage for persons under age 18 years and requires countries signing the charter to incorporate this into their laws.

It is critical to check which relevant international and regional human rights instruments a country has ratified. The Office of the United Nations High Commissioner for Human Rights maintains a worldwide database of the status of ratification of human rights instruments by country (www.ohchr.org). Another definitive source is the United Nations Treaty Section that maintains a register of multilateral treaties deposited with the Secretary-General (http://untreaty.un.org).

If a country has ratified the relevant international and regional human rights instruments, the country is obliged to integrate the content and spirit of the convention or treaty into national law, and the analysis that follows should capture how effectively this and the implementation of law has been. For example in the case of child marriage, it would be important to identify national (and state) laws governing marriage with specific attention paid to gender bias, minimum age of marriage, forcible marriage and rape, and dissolution of marriage. Depending on the country, knowing if birth registration and marriage registration is compulsory may be relevant, as well as how effectively the law is enforced if one exists.

If a country has not ratified relevant international or regional documents, the analysis should consider: the country's reasons for not participating in international or regional normative standards; whether existing national laws violate or uphold the international and regional standards, and; whether rights addressed in the UDHR (that although nonbinding contributes to customary law) are relevant to the topic. These steps will help frame the social issue from a rights-based perspective, either as a violation of rights or identifying the less than full realization of relevant rights. One may further explore whether the country has made general or specific reservations to the international human rights instruments it has ratified with regard to gender, age, traditional law or religion; or if reservations have been made to the definition of a child in CRC.

Consideration must be given to issues that span across two or more international human rights covenants. For example, in the case of child marriage, there are strong linkages to children's and women's rights as presented in the CRC and CEDAW. Child marriage may also affect the realization of rights articulated in the other covenants such as CERD, CM, or the CRPD. Complementary areas across treaties should reinforce advocacy and evaluating areas of conflict will lead to careful and comprehensive consideration. Going back to child marriage as the example, comparing the CRC and CEDAW on rights relevant to child marriage would be a good place to begin. Both include articles addressing the right to health, education, nationality, access state resources, rest and leisure, and equal treatment regardless of gender. They highlight parental responsibility to raise children, the state obligation to provide child care facilities, and emphasize the importance of considering the best interests of the child in decision making. The covenants are explicit about eliminating the trafficking of girls and women, protecting girls and women from sexual exploitation, and recognizing the necessity of private and public partnership. Subject to interpretation, the CRC however can be seen to emphasize girlhood as a conduit to motherhood compared to the emphasis in CEDAW to see women as whole human beings who may or may not be mothers.

The next step is to contextualize the social issue by understanding the cause(s) underlying the issue, the consequences of the social issue, who and what contributes to its perpetuation, and who is affected by the social issue (stakeholders). In the example of child marriage, household poverty and discriminatory cultural practices are at the root of the practice. Girls are seen as economic burdens to families in some cultures because they are expected to leave their birth families when they marry and contribute to the welfare of their husband's family. This often occurs in cultures that attribute higher social, economic, and cultural status to males and tend to minimize the ability of women to participate in decisions affecting herself, her children, the family, and the community. Too often, women's livelihood and status in society is entirely dependent on their marital status and/or male guardianship. Economic hardship of the household then might be the root cause; cultural factors may exacerbate and reinforce the continuation of child marriage.

At the heart of a rights-based approach is the creation of conditions for all individuals to engage in a participatory process that will ultimately expand their capabilities and freedoms respecting their dignity and those of others. Policies that expose inequities and impose solutions are not rights-based. Rights-based policies value both the process and outcomes, making sure to include affected populations in social policy outcomes as well as in the decision-making process. Cultural practices may conflict with the realization of human rights such as gender equality. When this occurs, the decisions should be left to the people to decide, provided those whose rights have historically been dismissed or violated have the opportunity to participate and affect the decision-making process. An unambiguous understanding of the beliefs and values of the people is important to inform policy decisions. Culture provides the contextual environment for human rights and ultimately facilitates the realization of human rights by allowing for ownership and debate of the issue.

The stakeholders in this issue will vary depending on the country and the cultural context but generally speaking they will include child brides and grooms; the fathers or male guardians responsible for negotiating marriages; mothers or female guardians who sometimes reinforce societal expectations or may take issue with the practice; other relatives who may act as gatekeepers for the family honor; and community practices that may dictate standards for bride prices or dowries dependent on age and status of the bride.

Following the identification of stakeholders, the ways in which each stakeholder benefits or loses from child marriage should be evaluated. Examples include economic gains and losses to families, the benefits and losses to the child bride or groom (education, physical or emotional abuse, labor division, securing a socioeconomic position within a society), and the benefits and losses to the community (social and economic development, reinforcing patriarchy and cultural practice, etc.). The duty bearers may include the parents, the husband, the in-laws, the community, the government, and possibly the media and other opinion makers who consciously shape public opinion on child marriage.

The next step is to consider how child marriage affects one or all four of the human rights principles of *participation, accountability, nondiscrimination, and equality (P.A.N.E.)*. In the case of child marriage, the principles of *nondiscrimination and equality* are violated because it has a differential impact on women and men, girls and boys. Boys may also be forced into child marriages but the prevalence is much higher among girls. Many countries legally recognize the marriage of males at age 18 and females at age 16. Girls are more likely to suffer physically because they may be encumbered with heavy physical tasks that are damaging, forced to have sexual relations prematurely, and experience lifelong physical suffering from bearing children early and continuously. Young girls who marry older men are at a higher risk for physical and mental abuse, and are more likely to get sexually transmitted infections such as HIV/AIDS. As a result of marriage, girls may forfeit their education (UNPF, 2012). The community and family may offer girls who marry young few options for recourse. The analysis could demonstrate the gender bias that is perpetuated by child marriage.

Another dimension to be considered in the analysis is who *participates* in and who is excluded from decisions affecting child marriage practices at the family, community, and legislative levels. One could analyze how marriage decisions are made and stem recommendations for changing the process and/or participants. Measuring participation in decision making can be daunting. For example, there is no standard method for measuring children's participation in society. A good place to begin is to review the legal provisions within a country allowing women and children to participate in decisions affecting their well-being, specifically around participation in marriage decisions. The analysis may include an evaluation of the children's minimum ages of consent; confidential mechanisms offered for women and children to express their own opinions, conscience and religion in accordance with evolving capacities; legal entitlements to be involved in decision-making processes affecting their lives and legal proceedings; and obligations to involve children in decisions affecting them and women more generally. If these mechanisms do exist, the analysis may explore the methods for making women and children aware of their legal rights and the mechanisms available to them including the process for children to exercise their rights. More generally, consideration should be given to opportunities available for women and children to influence local and national government legislation, policies, services, and resource allocations.

Accountability is closely related to access, a critical element in the human rights framework. In the event of a violation or denial of rights, a rights-based approach emphasizes the need to have available and appropriate means to seek and support redress, including invoking the right to remedy and to due process, and the right to information. The existence of mechanisms for redress should be included in an analysis as well as accessibility, availability, and affordability to these mechanisms. What structures and processes are in place for a child spouse to seek redress for rights violations in a marriage? Can a child present directly in court or must a representative be appointed for the child? Who and how is this represented appointed? What procedures are in place to assure the neutrality of the representative and safeguard the child from further repercussions? How are children made aware of the availability of such services? Are these processes transparent and if not, in what ways do they impede redress regarding child marriage?

Accountability also includes transparency. Transparency is a critical safeguard against corruption, exclusion, political favoritism, and an important means of facilitating access to and participation in rights realization. By not knowing the means available to influence policymaking, the resources that can be used and the information on an issue, the ability to claim one's rights is impeded. Policies and laws become vulnerable to those who interpret what can and cannot be done. Not only should legal, financial resources, and administrative processes be transparent and open to question, but they also should available in a language and at a level that is understandable to rights holders. A child who wants out of a marriage or does not want to marry should be able to understand where they can go to access help, the type of help available, and the options and consequences of one's choices. We all have the right to freedom of expression that includes the right to seek and receive information from the State (Sepúlveda & Nyst, 2012).

Policy recommendations flowing from this analysis should seek to address the violations or denial of rights identified in the first part of the analysis with consideration given to the stakeholders and their roles as duty bearers. The recommendations must identify the root cause of child marriage and responsibility for rectifying the rights violated by child marriage. If economic hardship is at the root of child marriage, the policy recommendations should consider alternative methods for securing household income that may reduce reliance on child marriage as an income source. In doing so, the recommendations should address how infringements of the human rights principles analyzed will be remedied by the proposed responses. Will laws be modified to address the discrimination revealed and unequal opportunities that result from the discriminatory practices? Will legislation be introduced to prohibit child marriage? What mechanisms will be introduced to enforce prohibition against child marriage? What will the response be to the likely resistance by some stakeholders? Do laws need to be introduced prohibiting gender-based violence and/or defining family violence? Do existing laws mandate minimum levels of education for children and do they need to be amended? What mechanisms are needed for redress to be accessible, available, and affordable to children who seek to end their marriages? If social protection programs are introduced to increase household livelihoods or human capital, the anticipated consequences on child marriage should be made clear and tied to the concerns identified by the analysis of the principles.

This case example yields information on the causes of child marriage and frames the issue in a way that calls for progressive responses that will further the realization of rights not just attend to the immediate causes to the problem. The approach utilized in this chapter relies on legal frames to identify specific and interrelated violations of rights. To develop policy recommendations that are responsive to the root causes requires a solid contextual understanding of the issue, the stakeholders involved and their perspectives, and a clear definition of the duty bearers. A deepened understanding of the social issue can be derived from analyses of how the issue compromises the four basic human rights principles: participation, accountability, nondiscrimination, and equality. By proposing policy recommendations that are responsive to the violations or denials of human rights principles, the recommendation should further the realization of rights.

It seems likely that the indicators needed for the proposed rights-based approach may not always be available and accessible, and their accuracy may be of question in some countries. This is the subject of the next chapter.

The rights-based approach to social policy analysis proposed here asks social workers to reinsert the value base that our profession was built upon by placing the furthering of human dignity and elimination of human suffering at the center of our practices. New solutions to old problems can only be achieved through innovative ways of understanding the social issues and consequent alternative approaches.

2.4 Suggested Exercise

Homelessness continues to be a national crisis in the United States, affecting 3.5 million people each year, including a rising number of families. In cities and towns around the country, homelessness is increasingly portrayed as a criminal activity. Nationwide, homeless people are targeted, arrested, and jailed under laws that criminalize homelessness by making it illegal for homeless persons to sit or stand in public spaces. The laws, designed to move visibly homeless people out of commercial and tourist districts or, increasingly, out of entire cities, are often justified as necessary public health and public safety measures. A review by the National Law Center on Homelessness recently found that over one-third of 187 US cities impose city-wide bans on public camping, 27 % of cities prohibit sleeping in particular public places, such as in public parks, 76 % of cities prohibit begging in particular public places, 65 % of cities have laws prohibiting loitering, loafing, and vagrancy in public places, 53 % of cities prohibit sitting or lying down in particular public places, 43 % of cities prohibit sleeping in vehicles, and 9 % of cities have laws prohibiting the sharing food with homeless people.[1] For most of homeless persons living in public spaces is the last option available to them. Mr. Smith's story reflects a common experience.

The Story of Lawrence Lee Smith

Smith became homeless after his degenerative joint disease made him no longer able to work in construction. He lived in a camper van for years until it was towed. He couldn't afford to retrieve it, leaving him with nowhere to reside but in public places in Boise, Idaho, due to frequent overcrowding of area homeless shelters. Mr. Smith was cited for illegal camping and was jailed for a total of 100 days. Due to the arrest, he lost his tent, his stove, and the fishing equipment he relied upon to live.

Criminalizing homelessness does nothing to address the underlying causes of homelessness and, instead, only worsens the problem. The arrest of homeless people is only a temporary intervention, as most are arrested and incarcerated for short periods of time thereafter returning to their communities, still with nowhere to live and bearing additional financial burdens such as legal fees that they cannot afford to pay. Their imprisonment adds additional barriers to obtaining critical public benefits, employment, or housing, thus further entrapping individuals within homelessness.

---

[1] For more information, see National Law Center on Homelessness& Poverty and Los Angeles Community Action Network (2014). Racial Discrimination in Housing and Homelessness in the United States: A Report to the UN Committee on the Elimination of Racial Discrimination. Retrieved from http://www.nlchp.org/documents/CERD_Housing_Report_2014.

Here are some suggested steps for guiding a rights-based analysis of homelessness policy.

- Beginning with the UDHR and moving to binding international and regional human rights instruments, is housing a human right? Is there a right to housing in the United States (or in another country of interest)? Document your sources in human rights and national laws and discuss areas of ambiguity regarding housing as a right.
- What other rights allowing for persons to be homeless might violate? Are there laws in the country of interest that directly or indirectly prohibit homelessness? Homelessness is a state. Homeless people may spend more time sitting or sleeping on benches in public spaces than average citizens, should these activities be viewed as criminal? Does your community have laws against public camping, sleeping in public places, begging in particular public places, loitering, loafing, and vagrancy in public places, sitting or lying down in particular public places, sleeping in vehicles, and sharing food with homeless people? Are these laws in accordance with international human rights and national laws?
- What is the root cause of homelessness? In what ways does or does not the criminalization of homeless address the root causes?
- In what ways do current laws regarding public spaces facilitate the realization or violate human rights?
- Identify the stakeholders in homelessness policy. Who are the rights holders? Who are the duty bearers?

Analyze laws on homeless use of public space according to cross-cutting human rights principles of participation, accountability, nondiscrimination, and equality (P.A.N.E.).

- Participation.
  Are rights holders and duty bearers given opportunities to be heard at every stage of the policymaking process regarding homeless policy? Are there groups who have been historically marginalized due to ethnicity, gender, language, or ability? How do rights holders participate in the policymaking process? In what ways are the voices of rights holders not included in the policymaking process? What are the challenges in including rights holders in the policymaking process, if any?
- Accountability.
  As duty bearers, states hold the responsibility of implementing laws, policies, and programs that further the realization of human rights in the country.
  - Does the state make information available and accessible in a timely manner on the progress of its efforts to address homelessness and public use policy?
  - If rights holders feel their rights are violated, is the process to challenge the decision documented and without repercussions? Are accountability mechanisms in place with responsibility of implementation clear and open to input from all?

- Nondiscrimination and equality.
  The State has the task of ensuring that all policies and practices relating to homelessness and use of public spaces are nondiscriminatory and that priority is given to protect the most vulnerable segments of the population. In what ways if any, is the policy discriminatory? Socially unjust? Consider, for example, that homeless persons of color have higher rates of being arrested and incarcerated than whites. The discriminatory impact of criminalization of homelessness was specifically pointed out by the Special Rapporteur on Racism during his 2008 visit to the United States, citing the example of Los Angeles' Skid Row.

2.4.1 In-Class Discussions

In Denmark and in other countries, homelessness is viewed as an alternative lifestyle. It is the responsibility of government to protect homeless persons from doing harm to themselves and others and the goal of public policies is to provide the supports needed for persons choosing to be homeless to live safely, rather than condemning their lifestyle choice. Is there a right to homelessness? What international, regional, and in-country laws support this? What do you think about public taxpayer dollars being spent on support a homeless lifestyle?

- Consider other stakeholders such as parents of young children who fear that a homeless person may carry disease or be unstable emotionally and thus are reluctant to bring their children to public parks. What policy responses would you recommend that account for the rights of the homeless and their use of public space? What are the rights of those who argue that homelessness infringes on their use and enjoyment of public spaces?
- What policy responses would you recommend that address the root causes of homelessness?

References

CEDAW Committee. (1989). General recommendation No. 12—eighth session, 1989 violence against women.

CEDAW Committee. (1992). General recommendation No. 19—eleventh session, 1992 violence against women.

Family Watch International. (2009). Family policy brief: ICESCR Committee General Comment 20. www.familywatchinternational.org.

Fee, E., & Parry, M. (2008). Jonathan Mann, HIV/AIDS, and human rights. *Journal of Public Health Policy, 29*(1), 54–71.

Hertel, S., & Libal, K. (2011). *Human rights in the United States: Beyond exceptionalism.* Cambridge, UK: Cambridge University Press.

Mann, J. M., Gruskin, S., Grodin, M. A., & Annas, G. J. (Eds.). (1999). *Health and human rights: A reader.* New York: Routledge.

Patterson, A. S. (2009). AIDS/HIV. In D. P. Forsythe (Ed.), *Encyclopedia of human rights*. Oxford, UK: Oxford University Press.

Petersen, C. (2011). Bridging the gap?: The role of regional and national human rights institutions in the Asia Pacific. *Asian-Pacific Law & Policy Journal, 13*(1), 174–209.

Sepúlveda, M., & Nyst, C. (2012). *The human rights approach to social protection*. Finland: Ministry of Foreign Affairs.

Shaw, M. N. (2003). *International Law* (5th ed.). Cambridge University Press.

Stainton, T. (2005). Empowerment and the architecture of rights based social policy. *Journal of Intellectual Disabilities, 9*(4), 287–296.

UNAIDS. (2013). Global report: UNAIDS report on the global AIDS epidemic 2013. Joint United Nations Programme on HIV/AIDS.

United Nations Children's Fund. (2009). *The state of the world's children 2009: Maternal and newborn health*. UNICEF.

United Nations Population Fund. (2012). *Marrying too young: End child marriage*. UNFPA. http://www.unfpa.org/public/home/publications/pid/12166.

Chapter 3
Measuring Progress on the Realization of Human Rights

Measurement is the first step that leads to control and eventually to improvement. If you can't measure something, you can't understand it. If you can't understand it, you can't control it. If you can't control it, you can't improve it.

—H. James Harrington

Anything can be measured. If a thing can be observed in any way at all, it lends itself to some type of measurement method. No matter how "fuzzy" the measurement is, it's still a measurement if it tells you more than you knew before. And those very things most likely to be seen as immeasurable are, virtually always, solved by relatively simple measurement methods.

—Douglas Hubbard, *How to Measure Anything*

A human rights indicator is specific information on the state or condition of an object, event, activity or outcome that can be related to human rights norms and standards; that addresses and reflects human rights principles and concerns; and that can be used to assess and monitor the promotion and implementation of human rights.

—OHCHR, *Human Rights Indicators Guide*, 2012, p. 16.

A human rights-based approach to social policy is a conceptual, normative framework based on international human rights standards that seeks to promote and protect human rights. In a rights-based approach, social policies are developed and implemented to promote human rights and the analysis of social policies evaluates rights holders' efforts and duty bearers' obligations toward fulfilling human rights including the effects of policies on inequalities and vulnerabilities among populations, and the disclosure of discriminatory practices and unjust distributions of power that impede and undermine human rights. In a rights-based approach to social policy, both the process of arriving at social policy goals, plans and programs, and the goals, plans, and programs themselves are the subjects for analyses according to the human rights-based dimensions. Finding valid and comprehensive indicators of policies promoting rights realization is challenging because of the multidimensional nature of rights and the importance of process and outcomes.

© Springer International Publishing Switzerland 2016
S. Gatenio Gabel, *A Rights-Based Approach to Social Policy Analysis*,
SpringerBriefs in Rights-Based Approaches to Social Work,
DOI 10.1007/978-3-319-24412-9_3

Measuring the success and failures of policies to promote human rights is an elusive endeavor in many ways. For one, measuring social policies against the realization of human rights is not counting or even describing human rights violations per se. Nor is it limited to the listing of public laws that uphold or counter rights. Rather, the rights approach aims to capture how social policies and programs have progressed, regressed, or had no effect on the realization of rights.

A human rights approach seeks to evaluate both the process and outcome of social policies attending to human rights principles of nondiscrimination, equality, participation and accountability, and the shifts in power and influence between the *rights holders* and *duty bearers*. Measuring processes is complicated and given our propensity to assess the efficiency of social policies rather than the process, our measures of process are less developed whether they focus on the inclusion of beneficiaries in the policymaking process, creating structures to make laws and policies accountable, building mechanisms for redress, building transparency into budgets and policymaking, capturing the effectiveness of accountability in practice not just in the law, etc.

Human rights indicators should capture what are believed to be the causal relationships among legal standards, processes, and outcomes. They should also reflect the extent to which the process to implement and realize human rights is participatory, inclusionary, empowering, nondiscriminatory, or accountable. To analyze these factors, data is needed to reflect the experiences of groups that have been marginalized to demonstrate exclusion yet few regularly collected databases disaggregate process and outcomes on the basis of sex, disability, ethnicity, religion, language, etc. For instance, if we were interested in analyzing discriminatory practices in the United States related to non-English speakers with disabilities in a region, we may be able to locate data that shows admission rates in US colleges or hiring rates according to ethnicity, disability, or gender but less likely to find data collected on the interaction of factors and the structural processes that reinforce these practices. Indicators on the process facilitating rights realization are less developed and for now the challenge is to locate indicators that best approximate human rights realization while we advocate for the institutionalization of more comprehensive measures.

One of the characteristics differentiating civil/political rights from social, economic, and cultural rights is that as a general rule, civil and political rights are expected to take immediate effect. The realization of political and civil rights tends to be measured by its presence or absence, such as a law, but may be further evaluated to see if it is administered and practiced in nondiscriminatory ways and equally across the population. Civil and political rights include the right to life and safety, the right to justice and a fair trial, the right to free expression, and the right to choose one's beliefs. In contrast, it is expected that economic, social, and cultural rights will be implemented progressively over time because states need to build systems to realize certain rights such as education and health (Table 3.1).

We should be able to measure how social policies contribute to the progressive realization of social, economic, and cultural rights. Our measures should account for baselines to measure the progressive realization. Countries with the gravest of

Table 3.1 Types of political, civil, social, economic, and cultural rights

Civil and political rights	Economic, social, and cultural rights
The right to:	Practice one's culture (language, dress,
Life	customs, food, identity)
Name	Religion
Nationality	Education
Assembly	Family
Association	Marry or not marry
Asylum	Childhood
Dignity, honor, reputation	Food
Non-discrimination	Health
Safety	Work
Participate in communal life and decision's	Choose one's employment
affecting one's welfare	Organize at work
Property	Leisure
Speech and other forms of expression	Work conditions
Territory	Social Security (cash, subsidies, vouchers, tax
Mobility	benefits, in-kind, etc.)
Due Process	Gender
Equal protection under the law	
Appeal/redress	
Free from torture	
Be tried as a juvenile	
Trial	

violations should be reinforced for passing laws upholding human rights they have yet to implement but not for indefinite time periods. And countries that have generally well-developed social protections for its citizenry should not be relieved of their responsibilities to do better for *all* their citizens and from searching for innovative ways to improve rights realization.

Compared to political and civil rights, compelling states to respect economic and social rights obligations is trickier for several reasons. Social, cultural, and economic rights are based on a respect for human dignity and they are not based on a theory prescribing behaviors, exchanges, processes, or specified outcomes. To begin with, many States have not ratified all human rights treaties or have ratified the conventions with reservations, including the International Covenant on Economic, Social and Cultural Rights (ICESCR). When a country ratifies a treaty, it is legally bound to comply with the provisions therein but it may express reservations. A reservation or declaration is a limitation on the commitment undertaken by the country and must be made at the time of ratification. States are obliged to uphold these rights within their own cultural and political contexts. It is also possible for a country not to ratify the main human rights treaty and to ratify the optional protocols. The United States has not ratified the CRC, yet it has ratified the Optional Protocol to the CRC on the sale of children, child prostitution, and child pornography, and Optional Protocol to the CRC on the involvement of children in armed conflict.

Cultural relativism claims that these rights must be interpreted within one's culture. How then do we react to cultural traditions that subjugate gender equality or purposely disrespect population subgroups, such as disallowing women to vote, drive vehicles, work outside the home, or relegate lower educational opportunities to those who are challenged to learn because of disabilities or historical marginalization? Is it our place as outsiders to challenge these cultural norms or to instigate criticism by introducing normative, universal standards? Human rights are legal and social constructs and by deeming them universal we allow ourselves to intervene and sometimes interfere within cultures.

Measuring progress on social, economic, and cultural rights should also reflect the processes that have been implemented to promote rights or those that stand it the way. Yet, the establishment of a community council to develop educational standards, a seemingly positive step, that only consists of male, religious leaders who are not informed about learning challenges may perpetuate inequalities and discriminatory practices.

Perhaps because of these conflicts inherent in the human rights approach, we lack credible and agreed upon indicators of progress to base assessments of a state's progress on economic, social, and cultural rights. Unlike guaranteeing the right of citizens to vote or to receive fair hearings, for example, social and economic rights are subject to interpretations by each state and their implementation is gradual. The Committee on Economic, Social and Cultural Rights (CESCR) General Comment No. 3, however, requires the following core obligations to take immediate effect:

- The obligation not to discriminate among people in the realization of a right;
- The obligation to work toward the full realization of rights in question (including developing deliberate strategies and programs to reach the most vulnerable and excluded persons);
- The obligation to monitor progress toward the realization of human rights including making redress mechanisms accessible and available (CESCR, 1991).

3.1   United Nations' Monitoring and Measures of Human Rights

The United Nations has used indicators to measure progress on human rights for years. The treaty bodies, special procedural mandates, and universal periodic reviews were established as monitoring mechanisms that rely on a wide range of indicators to perform their jobs. The UN committees charged with overseeing the various human rights treaties routinely request information of all sorts: from descriptions of legislation passed to documentation of conditions that may facilitate or impede the enjoyment of a right within a country. Some human rights indicators are explicitly mentioned in human rights treaties. For example, Article 10 of CEDAW cites the reduction of "female student dropout rates" and States are instructed by Article 12 of the ICESCR to reduce infant mortality rates. The CRC and ICPR both call for birth registration and the CRPD obligates states to keep statistics on persons with disabilities.

Let us look at the various UN offices, special bodies and mechanisms created to monitor human rights realization. The Office of the High Commissioner for Human Rights (OHCHR) was created 20 years ago to advance human rights throughout the world. Today OHCHR's thematic priorities are to strengthen international human rights mechanisms; enhance equality and counter discrimination; combat impunity and strengthen accountability and the rule of law; integrate human rights in development and in the economic sphere; widen the democratic space; and protect human rights in situations of conflict, violence, and insecurity. OHCHR is a department of the UN Secretariat and is headquartered in Geneva with New York and regional offices. It works with international human rights mechanisms and bodies to monitor and develop human rights standards.

In 2006, the Human Rights Council (HRC) was established. HRC is a subsidiary organ of the General Assembly and the principal intergovernmental human rights body. Based in Geneva, it consists of 47 representatives of member States who are elected by the General Assembly and is responsible for strengthening the promotion and protection of human rights around the globe and for addressing situations of human rights violations and make recommendations on them. It has the ability to discuss all thematic human rights issues and situations that require its attention throughout the year.

One of the main responsibilities of the HRC is to oversee the Universal Periodic Review (UPR). This is a State-driven, peer review mechanism that was introduced in 2006. During the UPR, States report their progress and challenges in implementing human rights in accordance with the UN Charter, the UDHR, the treaties ratified by a country, voluntary pledges, and commitments made by the State (e.g., national human rights policies and/or programs implemented); and applicable international humanitarian law. The UPR provides the opportunity for each State to declare what actions they have taken to improve and fulfill the human rights situations in their countries. All 193 member States of the United Nations have been reviewed. The ultimate aim of this mechanism is to improve the human rights situation in all countries and address human rights violations.

The reviews are conducted by the UPR Working Group that consists of the 47 members of the Council and allow for any UN Member State to take part in the discussion with the reviewed States. The documents on which the reviews are based are: (1) information provided by the State under review; (2) information contained in the reports of independent human rights experts and groups, known as the Special Procedures; (3) human rights treaty bodies, and other UN entities; and (4) information from other stakeholders including national human rights institutions and nongovernmental organizations. States may commit to developing statistical systems and methods for collecting data to evaluate their progress in realizing human rights as a result of UPR reviews.

An important part of the review is the interactive dialog between the State under review and other UN member States. During the dialog, member States are able to raise questions and make recommendations to the State under review about their progress on human rights and address specific human rights challenges. A report is then compiled by the Troika Rapporteurs (three Council members selected to facilitate the review) with the UPR Secretariat and the State under review. The report includes a record of the issues raised during the dialog and lists the recommendations made by other States. Once the UPR Working Group adopts the report, it goes onto the Council for adoption and may include responses from the State under review. In addition to the UPR, the HRC uses other "Special Procedures" to review human rights practices of all members of the United Nations.

As discussed in Chap. 2, each international human rights treaty has a committee of independent experts known as a *treaty body*. The treaty body monitors the implementation of the treaty. Each country that has signed and ratified a treaty must submit regular reports to the treaty body about the human rights situation in the country. Each committee's mandate is defined in the treaty it oversees or in a protocol to that treaty. The treaty bodies consist of independent, impartial members who are elected by the states parties to the treaty. The table below depicts the treaty and the corresponding body at the United Nations.

Treaty	Treaty body
International Covenant on Civil and Political Rights	Human Rights Committee
Convention against Torture and Other Cruel, Inhuman or Degrading Treatment	Committee against Torture (CAT)
Convention on the Elimination of All Forms of Discrimination Against Women	Committee on The Elimination of Discrimination against Women (CEDAW)
International Convention on the Elimination of All Forms of Racial Discrimination (ICERD) and may receive individual complaints against States parties that have made the relevant declaration under Article 14 of the ICERD	Committee on The Elimination of Racial Discrimination (CERD)
International Covenant on Economic, Social and Cultural Rights (ICESCR) and may receive individual complaints relating to States parties to the Optional Protocol to the ICESCR (entered into force in 2013)	Committee on Economic, Social and Cultural Rights (CESCR)
International Convention on the Protection of the Rights of All Migrant Workers and Members of Their Families	Committee on the Protection of the Rights of All Migrant Workers and Members of Their Families (CMW)
International Convention on the Rights of Persons with Disabilities	Committee on the Rights of Persons with Disabilities (CRPD)
International Convention for the Protection of All Persons from Enforced Disappearance	Committee on Enforced Disappearances (CED)
Convention on the Rights of the Child and its two protocols	Committee on the Rights of the Child (CRC)

Each of the committee bodies requires member States to submit periodic reports to the relevant treaty body on how the rights are being implemented.

In addition to State parties' report, the treaty bodies may receive information on a country's human rights situation from other sources, including national human rights institutions (NHRIs), civil society organizations (CSOs), both international and national, UN entities, other intergovernmental organizations, and professional groups, and academic institutions. Most committees allocate specific plenary time to hearing submissions from CSOs and UN entities. Based on information available, the relevant treaty body examines the report in the presence of a State party's delegation. The Committee then publishes its concerns and recommendations, referred to as "concluding observations."

For example, overseeing the monitoring and implementation of the ICESCR is the United Nations Committee on Economic, Social and Cultural Rights (CESCR) that requires states to submit periodic reports (the first is due two years after the adoption of the ICESCR and every five years thereafter). These reports are used to assess a country's commitment and progress on realizing social, economic, and cultural rights. The conundrum is that countries that have not ratified the ICESCR are not subject to review. And even for countries that have ratified, the Committee has few enforcement mechanisms beyond these reports. It can expose inadequate commitment or achievement to the international community but lacks the authority and tools to sanction the lack of progress or violations committed or other tools for enforcement.

Despite the obligation to report on their own progress, indicators of human rights progress are in nascent stages in most countries. Human rights monitors seek to identify and investigate the extent to which the reality of a given situation falls short of the standards set forth in international human rights law. The lack of ratification of treaties or violations is regularly cited.

The cultural, political, interpretive, and methodological factors challenge the ability to identify cross-country indicators allowing comparisons across countries and against normative standards. OHCHR developed a common methodological framework of indicators that can be applied and contextualized at a national level for monitoring civil and political rights and economic, social, and cultural rights (OHCHR, 2012). The framework recommends the development of *structural*, *process*, and *outcome* indicators. This configuration of indicators should help assess the steps being taken by States in addressing their obligations—from commitments and acceptance of international human rights standards (*structural* indicators) to efforts being made to meet the obligations that flow from the standards (*process* indicators) and on to the results of those efforts (*outcome* indicators).

The OHCHR framework does not offer a common list of indicators to be applied across all countries irrespective of their social, political, and economic development. Nor does it make a case for building a global composite measure for cross-country comparisons of the realization or enjoyment of human rights. It does provide guidance for the conceptual identification of contextually relevant and feasible indicators in compliance with international human rights norms and principles.

This approach for identifying human rights indicators allow States to assess their own progress in implementing human rights and compliance with the international treaties and also provide tools for civil society to monitor progress and ensure accountability. Indicators can assist national governments in implementing rights-based policy and substantiate cases argued by human rights advocates. Drawing upon OHCHR's work on indicators, this chapter turns to apply it to social protection policies of interest. In all cases, the search for indicators should begin with a solid understanding the right(s), the source(s) of the right(s), and the perceived violations or shortcomings of the existing realization of the right. The next step is to determine the types of indicators available that can be used for measuring change, its strengths and limitations, who has the data, and how it can be accessed.

Rights based analysis commonly uses qualitative and quantitative indicators. Quantitative indicators are usually expressed as numbers, percentages, or indices such as the multidimensional poverty index, the death rate for children under the age of 5, and the number of persons from a historically excluded population elected to serve in Congress or Parliament. Data for quantitative approaches is typically gathered from surveys and questionnaires. The use of quantitative data allows us to organize, summarize, and compare large amounts of information to be used for trend analysis, progress reports, and for identifying magnitude of an issue of interest.

Qualitative indicators measuring human rights can explain or provide more details on quantitative information collected or can describe a monitored or new situation. Typically qualitative methods are aimed at describing a specific context, event, process, population, or reasons behind behaviors or processes. Qualitative data generally expands understanding of an issue or problem through rich, descriptive detail. Common qualitative research methods include observation, one-on-one interviews, focus groups, and case studies.

It is common to combine both qualitative and quantitative approaches in a human rights approach. For example, you may want to count the number of international treaties ratified by a country (quantitative information) and estimate the population adversely affected by a current policy but then describe how the treaty is being implemented differently across populations from data collected through focus groups (qualitative information). Quantitative and qualitative indictors can complement one another or be presented separately measuring different attributes.

The OHCHR framework begins by selecting *structural indicators* — indicators that assess the intent and commitment of a State to live up to the human rights obligations it has incurred. Often they reflect the ratification and adoption of legal instruments as well as the creation of basic institutional mechanisms to protect and promote human rights. It is also important to know if a government's ratification was with reservation status for each of the relevant treaties.

Some common structural indicators are:

- A State's ratification of international and regional human rights treaties;
- Existence, scope, and nature of domestic laws (or a domestic bill of rights in a State's constitution) with regard to specific rights;
- An assessment a national social policy regarding the promotion and protection of relevant rights including a time frame for implementation, coverage, availability, implementation strategy, etc.;
- Government accountability for its acts of commission or omission on rights implementation such as periodic reports, a national human rights institution, and civil society involvement in human rights monitoring.

Many of these structural indicators are likely to be used in a country's UPR. To see the UPR report submitted by the United States in 2015 go to www.state.gov/j/drl/upr/ and for civil society stakeholder recommendations see http://www.upr-info.org/database/. Other country reports, civil society, responses and country comments can be viewed at http://www.upr-info.org/database/.

Using the framework analysis discussed in this book, P.A.N.E. (participation, accountability, nondiscrimination, and equity)—we look to see if the human rights structural indicators incorporate the basic principles of the framework. To understand how the laws or policies were enacted, we would want to understand who *participated* in the decision making and who was not included. To do this we would need to understand how was the policy developed, who are the stakeholders, and if and how were they part of the process. Were there barriers to stakeholder participation? Were they overcome and how?

Next, we seek indicators to analyze how the legislation, constitution, or ratified treaties ensure *accountability*. How is the state held accountable for the policy under analysis? Is it legislated? Are the responsibilities of agents of the state specified? Who is responsible and at what levels of government for implementing the policy? Are evaluations mandated? Who performs the evaluations and how are results disseminated? What could be done to improve accountability and access to evaluative data?

We would then consider if the laws/constitution/treaty were *nondiscriminatory* and *equitable*. We would seek indicators to tell us if the national, state, and local laws reinforce the government's obligation regarding the social policy being analyzed? Do the indicators reference specific groups, say those who have been historically marginalized? Will the indicators be able to show how policy as written in law overcomes barriers? The analysis should include consideration of gender equality as appropriate (Fig. 3.1).

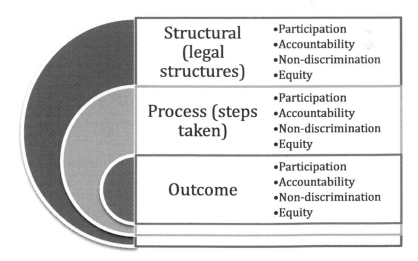

Fig. 3.1 Types of indicators

An analysis should not only identify relevant treaties and laws, but it should also consider at least one of the P.A.N.E. principles. For instance, how might we go about analyzing a country's child welfare policies. Historically, child welfare systems have been used to perpetuate and strengthen existing power relationships within a country. For example, between 25 and 35 % of American Indian children were removed from their families and placed in non-Indian mainstream homes over several decades (Unger, 1977). It was argued that this was being done in the best interest of the child (Article 6 of the CRC) since many of the children were living in poverty and raised according to Native American cultural traditions that are based on extended family rather than nuclear family attachments. American Indian representatives argued that the alarmingly high removal rate of Indian children threatened tribal survival. As a result, Congress enacted the Indian Child Welfare Act of 1978 to protect the best interests of Indian children, tribal survival and culture, and to promote the stability of Indian tribes and families (Unger, 1977). Other groups, including Roma children in Eastern Europe and children with disabilities throughout the world, have been subject to similar transgressions perpetuated by child welfare systems.

Table 3.2 summarizes the types of structural, process, and outcome indicators that may be used and the types of questions to be considered when searching for indicators to conduct a P.A.N.E. analysis.

Process indicators continually assess the specific measures that duty bearers take to implement the commitments to human rights implementation. Whereas structural indicators are more likely to be event driven actions that put into place a structure for human rights realization, process indicators assess ongoing efforts. These measures may include the implementation of governance structures for accessibility and coverage, budget allocations, development programs, redress mechanisms, educating populations on human rights and its mechanisms, and functions of rights relevant institutions. Process indicators capture the progressive realization of rights and ongoing efforts of a State.

Using child welfare proceedings as the example, the process indicators using P.A.N.E. should locate the methods by which the voice of children is heard in proceedings such as child welfare custody or placement hearings. Child participation in child welfare decisions can take myriad forms: speaking to a guardian *ad litem* or Court Appointed Special Advocate (CASA) or social worker/clinician who will represent the child's interests in court; writing a letter to the judge, being present at court or in family meetings, meeting with or testifying before a judge, actively directing the decision-making process through the contribution of expressed wishes and identified needs to those who share the decision-making process, or having someone represent the views of a child (Donelly, 2010; Gallagher, Smith, Hardy, & Wilkinson, 2012; Jordan, 2009; Pinkney, 2011; Pitchal, 2008; Skivenes & Strandbu, 2006). Despite existing laws, participation efforts of children in matters that directly relate to their own welfare are inconsistent and infrequent, and typically fail to rise to the level of a child-centered or child-driven process (Donelly, 2010; Jordan, 2009; Pinkney, 2011; Pitchal, 2008; Skivenes & Strandbu, 2006).

Table 3.2 Guideline for selection of structural, process, and outcome indicators using P.A.N.E.

	Examples of general indicators	Participation	Accountability	Non-discrimination and equity
Structural	International and regional human rights treaties ratified Constitutional and legal provisions Public policies Institutional framework	How was the policy developed? Were concerned stakeholders, including specifically rights holders, consulted? Which aspects of accessibility are covered by the policy? E.g., physical and financial Does the policy include provisions to raise awareness about its content?	Does the national (and/or state if relevant) constitution address the obligation of the state regarding the social policy being studied? If so, describe and consider weaknesses as well strengths Which institutions and at what levels are responsible for administering and implementing programs, benefits, and services relevant to the social policy studied? Are the implementation responsibilities spread across more than one agency? If so, identify issues that arise from multiple administration of the issue regarding persons covered, served, excluded, eligibility criteria and requirements, benefit requirements, compliance, etc. Are there mechanisms in place for interagency coordination at national, regional, and local levels that could play a facilitating role for policy coherence? If so, describe	Which national, state, and local laws reinforce the government's obligation regarding the social policy being analyzed? Does the policy make reference to specific groups and or exclude others? On what basis have they been selected? Does the policy foresee the adoption of measures to counter prejudices and negative stereotypes preventing certain groups from accessing the benefits and services?

(continued)

Table 3.2 (continued)

	Examples of general indicators	Participation	Accountability	Non-discrimination and equity
Process	Public expenditures Coverage Complaints and redress Accessibility and affordability	What is the process for challenging government decisions regarding levels of benefits or services? Is the mechanism for redress accessible to all persons? What barriers might exist for certain groups? What is the process for obtaining budget information? Are hearings held for citizens to voice their opinions regarding budget priorities? Are potential beneficiaries able to participate in hearings regarding policymaking and regulations? Are the hearings accessible?	What is the level and/or percent of national/state/local budget allocated for this purpose? How has the level of expenditures changed over the last few years? In what areas, if any, have expenditures increased/decreased? Who has been affected by the change in the level of expenditures? Which are the institutions monitoring the service provision to persons with disabilities, minorities, indigenous, women, and migrants? Have complaints or citizen challenges increased or decreased over time? What may be some of the reasons contributing to the trend?	If contributions are required for receipt of benefits or services, which groups are included and which groups are (intentionally or otherwise) excluded? Are the criteria similar between men and women? Are benefits or services provided to excluded or marginalized groups by another program? If so, are the benefits to the excluded group equitable to the benefits provided to the covered group?

| Outcomes | Trend data on the proportion of population achieving milestones such as high school or college graduation, parenthood, employment
Trend data on the proportion of population experiencing specific rights violations
Comparative statistics on outcomes for marginalized and majority groups
Reports of systematic abuse or discrimination
Trend data on the proportion of population receiving benefit or services such as pensions, parental leave, counseling | Do beneficiaries of the social policy studied feel that their needs were taken into account in the development and implementation of the policy?
Do citizens feel they have control over their lives?
Do marginalized and vulnerable individuals feel that most people can be trusted or that you need to be very careful in dealing with people? | Have the preferences and/or needs of unserved groups been heard by government?
Why are the preferences/needs being unserved?
Are evaluations of social policy accessible to all? Do the mechanisms for distribution pose barriers to accessibility for certain groups, e.g., beneficiaries? | In what ways have certain groups benefited disproportionately from a social policy?
How has the inadequacy or lack of social policy in an area disadvantaged certain groups compared to others?
Who is disadvantaged by current policies or the lack of social policies?
What disparities exist between groups?
How have past policies impacted specific sectors of society? |

In some cases, children's participation may conflict with another CRC principle that requires all state actions be taken with the best of interests of the child in mind. Acting within its societal constructs of childhood, an agent of the state may represent the care needed for a child in accordance with how the state views the child's best interest which may be in conflict with a child's expressed preference or concerns. For example, a survey found that in the United States, 17 states provide no legal requirement to incorporate or advocate for the child's expressed view, emphasizing instead the "best interests" which may not align with the child's beliefs and wishes (RCW, 2005). Furthermore, a majority of US states utilize a framework in which representatives of children before the court may be expected to both represent the best interests of the child and the child's views, and the majority offer no guarantee to the child that they may be present and involved in court decisions. Likewise, efforts to protect children may obscure or hamper children's voiced preferences.

In this example, indicators should reflect the avenues available for children's voices to be heard, how and if governments are ensuring children have access to express their views in child welfare proceedings, and whether all children are heard equally or if the voices of some are ignored and why.

The third set of indicators is *outcome indicators*. Outcome indicators capture the effects of structural and process indicators over a period of time. These indicators reveal the realization of a right at a certain point in time and should be used against a baseline measure over time. Outcome measures are generally the last of the indicators to encapsulate changes. For example, treaties ratified and changes to laws against domestic violence can be identified and classified; and systems in place for persons to seek justice and help for violence committed against them or family members can also be reported and the status can be recorded. However, measuring the effects of the changes in laws and practice is far more challenging. If only ten women came forward in the past year to seek shelter from domestic violence, we are unlikely to assume that all women who have experienced domestic violence are seeking assistance. We would want to know if the number of women were more than the previous year or less, and we are more likely to question the barriers still in place that prevent more women from coming forward whether they be cultural, geographical, language, lack of information, cost, fear, etc. In this sense, more time will be needed to measure the realization of the right in an outcome indicator than it would to report on progressive reforms through structural and process indicators.

Outcome indicators are often used to assess multiple changes. These indicators may be based on data collected by governments, NGOs, researchers for another purpose but can also be used as a yardstick for rights realization. Measuring educational levels across a population can be an indicator of improvements to educational quality, availability, accessibility, or child well-being due to cultural shifts about educating girls or other children, income and/or health care delivery changes. Likewise, increases in child abuse reporting may be due to higher levels of stress in a society due to conflict, economic or political insecurity, or to new laws and processes that increase awareness of child abuse and changes in mandated reporting.

Examples of outcome indicators are gender equity, health status indicators, reports of rights violations, wealth and income distribution across and within populations (such as the Gini coefficient that measures the distribution of household consumption expenditure or income, incarceration rates, educational levels, and crime rates within and across populations).

The ability to separate data among subgroups is important for outcome indicators seeking to capture discrimination such as by sex, disability, ethnicity, religion, language, social, or regional affiliation. For instance, persons with disabilities have traditionally remained among the most hidden and neglected in education; in some circumstances they are "invisible" to education and to mainstream assistance. Students living with a disability usually experience exclusion, discrimination, and segregation in their access to mainstream education; and there has been a tendency to isolate children with disabilities from their peers, placing them in separate classes or in special schools. In some cases, children with disabilities have been refused education despite the 1993 UN Standard Rules on the Equalization of Opportunities of Persons with Disabilities that states that persons with disabilities should be entitled to access integrated school settings, extending this right to providing services in the community so that they can reside in their own communities (UNESCO, 2001). Proving exclusion is difficult if data cannot be disaggregated by presence of disability and type. The United Nations Statistics Division is currently working with countries to encourage measuring the incidence of disabilities by sex and age in the population censuses as part of efforts to implement socially inclusive social policies.

Referring back to the child welfare example, the outcome indicator in a policy analysis of child participation in child welfare proceedings should capture which children participate in proceedings or which do not, the effectiveness of current mechanisms in ensuring children's opinions are represented, and the obstacles preventing the voices of children from being heard. The effects of participation on children's well-being (e.g., Are children more likely to become self-sufficient as adults if they were able to express themselves as children in matters affecting their placement?) while interesting, important and tempting, stray from attempting to capture the of rights realization.

Depending on the problem chosen for assessment, a number of specific human rights may be affected, and these may influence the type of information you need to collect. The first step is to make a rough assessment of the availability or absence of indicators around the rights involved in the policy you are assessing according to the availability of structural, process, and outcome indicators. Use the following guide to help you in your choice of indicators.

Structural Indicators

1. Frame the social issue from a rights-based approach.
2. Identify the key human rights that states are obligated to protect as it relates to the social issue.
3. Identify relevant international human rights treaties pertaining to the social issue including the date of entry into force (the date the treaty went took effect),

coverage of the right(s) identified, and how multiple human rights may intersect over a single issue. For example, domestic violence not only violates a woman's right to be free from discrimination and violence (CEDAW, General Recommendation 19), it also triggers a woman's right to be free from torture (ICCPR), a woman's right to equality before the law (ICCPR), and a woman's right to the highest attainable standard of physical and mental health (ICESCR).
4. Review other policy documents that help interpret binding treaties, such as General Recommendations and Conclusions issued by the treaty bodies, as well as declarations, resolutions, principles, and guidelines (which may represent international consensus on an issue or influence practice).
5. Know the country's ratification and reservation status for each of the relevant treaties in order to obtain a clear sense of where a country stands on an issue and why.
6. Become familiar with the country's laws, plans, and regulations relevant to the issue.
7. Consider the ability of indicators available to capture P.A.N.E.

Process Indicators

1. What civil, criminal, and administrative processes address relevant human rights issues?
2. What agencies, offices, or actors are involved?
3. What plans, policies, and protocols have been issued regarding or relevant to the social issue of interest?
4. Consider the ability of indicators available to capture P.A.N.E.

Outcome Indicators

1. Assuming the progressive realization of a right will affect the well-being of persons involved, the indicator or indicators chosen should reflect linkage or a causal relationship.
2. Outcome indicators should be culturally relevant and accepted by the relevant culture.
3. Does the indicator reflect evidence about who benefits (and does not) from current interventions, policies, or procedures perpetuating discriminatory structure and practices, or exclusion from protection that facilitates one's rights? Administrative data for example, may indicate who is being served but may not capture who is omitted. On the other hand, survey data may not include information on eligibility, processes, etc.
4. Consider the availability, validity, and reliability of an indicator to establish a baseline demonstrating an outcome prior to a policy or plan was implemented (or in early stages of implementation) and then to reflect subsequent changes over time. If possible, data collected should be recurrent.
5. Does the indicator considered reflect the cumulative effects of the processes involved?
6. Is disaggregated data available for a particular group of interest? If not, is it possible to request or estimate based on existing data?
7. Consider the ability of indicators available to capture P.A.N.E.

The information sought clearly goes beyond seeking statistics. For instance, with regard to the right to just and favorable conditions of work (an economic or social right), the ILO asks: "What procedures exist to ensure that men and women are actually paid equal remuneration for equal work? Do, for instance, equal opportunities commissions exist? By whom are they staffed, and to what extent are they independent?" (as cited in Green, 2001).

3.2 Sources for Indicators

In the United States, there are a large number and array of data sources publicly accessible. Here, a sampling of sources that could be used related too health and well-being.

Partners in Information Access for the Public Health Workforce http://phpartners.org/

MedlinePlus http://medlineplus.gov/

HSS Data Council Gateway to Data and Statistics—Federal Government http://aspe.hhs.gov/statinfo/

Statistical Abstract of the United States—U.S. Census Bureau http://www.census.gov/statab/www/

FedStats Federal Government http://www.fedstats.gov/

State & County QuickFacts—U.S. Census Bureau—Federal Government http://quickfacts.census.gov/qfd/

Statistical Resources on the Web—University of Michigan http://www.lib.umich.edu/govdocs/stats.html

*State Health Facts Online—*Kaiser Family Foundation http://www.statehealthfacts.kff.org/

3.2.1 Federal Government Health Statistics Agencies

National Center for Health Statistics (NCHS) http://www.cdc.gov/nchs/

Agency for Healthcare Research and Quality (AHRQ) http://www.ahrq.gov/

Substance Abuse and Mental Health Services Administration (SAMHSA) http://www.samhsa.gov/

Centers for Medicare and Medicaid Services (CMS) http://www.cms.gov/

3.2.2 National Library of Medicine

*Health Data Tools and Statistics—*Partners in Information Access for the Public Health Workforce http://phpartners.org/health_stats.html

Health Services and Sciences Research Resources (HSRR) — National Information Center on Health Services Research and Health Care Technology (NICHSR) http://www.nlm.nih.gov/nichsr/hsrr_search/
Toxicology and Environmental Health — Specialized Information Services http://sis.nlm.nih.gov/Tox/ToxMain.html

3.2.3   Agency for Healthcare Research and Quality

HCUP — *Healthcare Cost and Utilization Project* http://www.ahcpr.gov/data/hcup/
MEPS — *Medical Expenditure Panel Survey* http://www.meps.ahrq.gov/default.htm

3.2.4   Centers for Disease Control and Prevention (CDC)

Behavioral Risk Factor Surveillance System (BRFSS) http://www.cdc.gov/brfss/
National Health Care Survey (NHCS) http://www.cdc.gov/nchs/nhcs.htm
National Health Interview Survey (NHIS) http://www.cdc.gov/nchs/nhis.htm
National Health and Nutrition Examination Survey (NHANES) http://www.cdc.gov/nchs/nhanes.htm
National Immunization Survey http://www.cdc.gov/nip/coverage/default.htm#NIS
National Notifiable Disease Surveillance System (NNDSS) http://www.cdc.gov/epo/dphsi/nndsshis.htm
National Vital Statistics System http://www.cdc.gov/nchs/nvss.htm
Youth Risk Behavior Surveillance System (YRBSS) http://www.cdc.gov/nccdphp/dash/yrbs/index.htm

3.2.5   Substance Abuse and Mental Health Services Administration

National Survey on Drug Use & Health (formerly called the National Household Survey on Drug Abuse) http://www.samhsa.gov/oas/nhsda.htm
Drug Abuse Warning Network (DAWN) http://dawninfo.samhsa.gov/
Drug and Alcohol Services Information System (DASIS) http://www.samhsa.gov/oas/dasis.htm#DASISinfo
Alcohol and Drug Services Study (ADSS) http://www.samhsa.gov/oas/adss.htm

3.2.6   Centers for Medicare and Medicaid Services (CMS)

Acute Inpatient Prospective Payment System http://cms.hhs.gov/providers/hipps/default.asp

Cost Data Sets http://cms.hhs.gov/data/download/default.asp
Medicare Current Beneficiary Survey (MCBS) http://www.cms.hhs.gov/MCBS/
   default.asp

3.2.7   Other National and State Organization Sources

Behavioral Risk Factor Surveillance System (BRFSS) http://www.cdc.gov/brfss/
Child Stats—Federal Interagency Forum on Child and Family Statistics http://
   www.childstats.gov/
FEDSTATS—Federal government http://www.fedstats.gov/
State & County QuickFacts—U.S. Census Bureau http://quickfacts.census.gov/qfd/
State and Local Area Integrated Telephone Survey—CDC http://www.cdc.gov/
   nchs/slaits.htm
State Health Departments—CDC http://www.cdc.gov/mmwr/international/relres.
   html
State Profiles—Children's Defense Fund http://www.childrensdefense.org/states/
   state_profiles.htm
State Health Facts Online—Kaiser Family Foundation http://www.statehealthfacts.
   kff.org/
Statistics for Cities and Other Places—U.S. Census Bureau http://www.census.
   gov/epcd/www/places.htm

3.2.8   International Sources

For those interested in comparative or international work, the following sites may
   prove useful.
United Nations Statistics Division—http://unstats.un.org/unsd/
World Bank Group Data and Statistics—http://www.worldbank.com/data/
World Health Organization—Statistical Information System (WHOSIS) http://
   www3.who.int/whosis/menu.cfm
UNESCO Statistics—http://stats.uis.unesco.org/unesco/tableviewer/document.
   aspx?ReportId=143
World Data on Education from International Bureau of Education (IBE)—http://
   www.ibe.unesco.org/International/Databanks/Wde/profilee.htm
FAO Statistical Databases—http://www.fao.org/corp/statistics/en/
Labor Statistics Database at International Labor Organization (ILO)—http://laborsta.
   ilo.org/
African Development Bank Statistics—http://www.afdb.org/en/knowledge/statistics/
Asian Development Bank Statistics—http://www.adb.org/Statistics/default.asp
Inter-American Development Bank Statistics—http://www.iadb.org/research/statis-
   tics.cfm?lang=en

International Internet Domain Survey (Network Wizards)—https://www.isc.org/solutions/survey

World Resources Institute Statistical Data Tables—http://pubs.wri.org/pubs_content_text.cfm?ContentID=2460

Association of Southeast Asian Nations Statistics—http://www.aseansec.org/22122.htm

Asian-Pacific Economic Cooperation Member Economy Data Files—http://www.apec.org/apec/member_economies.html

Statistical Profile of Education in sub-Saharan Africa (SPESSA)—http://www.eldis.org/assets/Docs/25934.html

Population Reference Bureau Datafinder—http://www.prb.org/datafinder.aspx

Pan American Health Organization (PAHO)—http://www.paho.org/

United Nations Population Information Network—http://www.un.org/popin/data.html

World Population Prospects Online Database—http://esa.un.org/unpp/

UN Statistics Division—http://www.un.org/depts/unsd/index.html

UNSTATS Common Database—http://unstats.un.org/unsd/cdb/cdb_help/cdb_quick_start.asp

Human Development Reports—http://www.undp.org/hdr2001/

UNCEF Statistics on Children—http://www.unicef.org/statis/index.html

UNHCR Annual Statistics on Refugees—http://www.unhcr.org/pages/49c3646c4d6.html

The World's Women: Statistical Tables—http://unstats.un.org/unsd/demographic/products/Worldswomen/WWreports.htm

UNCJIN International Crime and Justice Statistics—http://www.uncjin.org/Statistics/WCTS/wcts.html

3.2.9 European Union and Advanced Economy Country Statistical Systems

EUROSTAT: Official Statistical Office of European Union—http://epp.eurostat.ec.europa.eu/portal/page/portal/eurostat/home/

European Union Agency for Safety and Health at Work Statistics—http://europe.osha.eu.int/statistics/

European Monitoring Centre for Drugs and Drug Addiction Data Library—http://ar2003.emcdda.europa.eu/en/page084-en.html

Statistics from the European Observatory on the Social Situation, Demography and Family—http://ec.europa.eu/employment_social/spsi/european_observatory_en.htm

Organisation for Economic Co-operation and Development (OECD)—http://www.oecd.org/home/

SourceOECD: The OECD's Online Library of Books, Periodicals, and Statistics—
    http://lysander.sourceoecd.org/vl=6015415/cl=11/nw=1/rpsv/home.htm
*UN Economic Commission for Europe Statistics—*http://w3.unece.org/pxweb/
    Dialog/

3.3   Class Exercises

3.3.1   Do Older Americans Have a Right to Long Term Care?

Few people have insurance that protects them against the potential costs of long-term services and supports, such as personal assistance at home, assisted living services, or nursing home care. Medicare covers short-term post-acute care, but does not pay for long-term stays in a nursing home or other facility. Medicaid benefits include long-term services and supports, but only for people with low financial resources, including those who have exhausted their resources paying for medical care and long-term services and supports. Private long-term care insurance is designed to pay for long-term care services, but only about 10 % of seniors have this type of insurance. The cost of long-term care insurance is a significant barrier to take up, with a typical premium for a couple (both age 60) around $3000 per year and rising considerably with age.

Most seniors live on low or modest incomes. Nearly 1 in 10 seniors had family income below the federal poverty threshold ($10,458 for single individuals age 65 or older and $13,194 for senior couples) in 2010, and 35 % had incomes less than twice the poverty threshold. When out-of-pocket medical expenses are considered, the share of seniors living in poverty in 2010 increases from 9.0 to 16 %. In 2010, the top 10 % of Medicare beneficiaries ages 65 and older had annual incomes of $65,000 or greater, while the top 5 % had annual incomes of $86,100 or greater.

Despite low rates of long-term care coverage, two-thirds of those ages 65 and over are projected to need some long-term services and supports during their lifetimes, and an estimated 18 % will use more than one year of nursing home care during the remainder of their lives. Extensive services in a nursing home or assisted living facility or at-home care can quickly go through any savings. The annual cost of nursing home care, for example, averaged about $78,000 nationwide in 2011 for a semiprivate room, and over $100,000 annually in several of the most expensive areas—well in excess of the median savings of older persons which averaged $66,900 in 2010. Because the cost of these services can add up quickly, low- and middle-income persons with extensive long-term care needs often deplete their savings paying for care and many become eligible for Medicaid coverage. About one-third of Medicaid spending covers long-term services and supports.

In the end, after private and family supports have been exhausted, the public through Medicaid will provide long term care services for individuals.

Using the framework outlined in this chapter, what types of structural, process, and outcome indicators might you use to analyze current long term care policy?

Hints: There is no treaty addressing the human rights of older persons—how does this affect your interpretation of long term care as a right? What treaties can be used to argue for/against long term care as a right?

In effect, the US policy (Medicaid for the poor and private provision for those who can afford to purchase it) leaves out the majority of middle-class Americans? Is this discriminatory? Who benefits from the current policy and who is left out?

3.3.2 *Evil or Miracle Drug? Who Decides and How?*

For most of the history of the United States, cannabis was legal and commonly found in tinctures and extracts. This is in contrast to views of cannabis for the latter half of the twentieth century when it was largely viewed as dangerous, the gateway drug, the assassin of youth, the killer weed, marijuana. But in this century, increasing numbers of people are turning to cannabis as a drug that can help certain medical conditions and symptoms, some even refer to it as a new miracle drug. It is now being used legally and otherwise as a pain killer, sleep aid, appetite stimulant, stress reliever, analgesic, antiemetic, bronchodilator, anti-inflammatory, protector against brain trauma, and immune system booster. It is used to treat symptoms related to glaucoma, multiple sclerosis, cancer, and AIDS. But it can increase carbon dioxide intake, increase the risk of heart attacks in some, and make it difficult to regulate food intake.

In the United States, 23 states and the District of Columbia have legalized cannabis for medical uses and a majority of Americans favor legalization for recreational uses. It is now legal in Uruguay, Portugal has decriminalized it and several countries including Canada, the Netherlands, and Israel have medical marijuana programs.

For students to consider: Is cannabis an evil or miracle drug? Should it be legalized? For those who choose to be consumers, is it their right? What about the negative effects often cited as cannabis leading to other, more harmful drug usage? Its association with crime? Delinquency?

Divide the class into groups. One group should take the position that cannabis is a human right. The second group should be against the legalization of cannabis. The third group should act as representing the public interest and decide what type of indicators should be used to decide whether cannabis should be legalized. All groups should use a rights-based approach. The purpose is to think about the types of indicators that could be used.

All groups should situate cannabis within a human rights and P.A.N.E. framework to identify the structural, process, and outcome indicators. Consideration should be given to the availability and accessibility of the indicators. Groups one and two should choose indicators to support their position. Group three should consider which indicators (regardless) of position are valid and reliable, noting the shortcomings (e.g., not regularly collected data, lack of data disaggregation, data only available for certain groups or regions, and anecdotal) where appropriate.

Depending on time available, the groups reconvene to present their cases to the third group who decides based on the merit of the evidence presented, who has a stronger case (for or against) and why.

References

Committee on Economic, Social and Cultural Rights. (1991). General Comment 3, The nature of States parties' obligations (Fifth session, 1990), U.N. Doc. E/1991/23, annex III at 86.

Donelly, C. (2010). Reflections of a *Guardian Ad Litem* on the participation of looked-after children in public law proceedings. *Child Care in Practice, 16*(2), 181–193.

Gallagher, M., Smith, M., Hardy, M., & Wilkinson, H. (2012). Children and families' involvement in social work decision making. *Children & Society, 26*, 74–85.

Green, M. (2001). What we talk about when we talk about indicators: Current approaches to human rights measurement. *Human Rights Quarterly, 23*, 1062–1097.

Jordan, K. (2009). Need to be heard: Increasing child participation in protection mediation through the implementation of model standards. *Family Court Review, 47*(4), 715–736.

Office of the High Commissioner on Human Rights (OHCHR). (2012). *Human rights indicators: A guide to measurement and implementation.* New York: United Nations.

Pinkney, S. (2011). Participation and emotions: Troubling encounters between children and social welfare professionals. *Children & Society, 25*, 37–46.

Pitchal, E. S. (2008). Where are all the children? Increasing youth participation in dependency hearings. *UC Davis Journal of Juvenile Law and Policy, 12*(1), 233–262.

Representing Children Worldwide (RCW). (2005). How children's voices are heard in child protective proceedings. Retrieved from http://www.law.yale.edu/rcw/rcw/jurisdictions/am_n/usa/united_states/frontpage.htm#_ednref12.

Skivenes, M., & Strandbu, A. (2006). A child perspective and children's participation. *Children, Youth, and Environments, 16*(2), 10–27.

UNESCO. (2001). *Open file on inclusive education support: Materials for managers and administrators.* Paris: Inclusive Education Section for Combating Exclusion through Education, Division of Basic Education.

Unger, S. (1977). *The destruction of American Indian families.* New York: Association on American Indian Affairs.

Chapter 4
Bringing It All Together

Amber T. has worked in a medical practice that offers no paid maternity leave benefits for years. Amber's first child was born when Amber was 19 years old and she wasn't married. She took 3 weeks off, two of which were her accrued vacation time and one without pay. Amber then married and a couple of years later she was able to take 5 weeks off when her son was born. She again used 2 weeks of saved vacation time and 3 weeks were unpaid leave. Amber works in a small office that is not covered under the Family Medical Leave Act. Amber's husband works as a contractor for a small company who offer no paternity leave. Amber wanted to take additional time off to be with her infant son and toddler daughter yet the family's finances were strained by the 3 weeks unpaid leave she took and the bills and credit card balances were building up. She asked her employer if she could return to work part-time and he reluctantly agreed. Amber's co-workers resented the time she took during her limited days at work to pump breast milk and told her employer they needed a full-time person in the position. Amber agreed to return full-time but her employer and her co-workers soon after lost patience with Amber's unstable child care arrangements and she was let go. The family debt increased, their savings diminished and family relationships were strained. Amber was forced to confront the possibility of her marriage ending and becoming a single-mother on public assistance.

In this chapter, we use a social issue and analyze it from the rights-based framework presented earlier. We will look at the parental and family leave policies in the United States and the effects current policies have on women such as Amber and their families. Current family leave policies in the United States too often forsake women like Amber who aim to be nurturing mothers, stable partners, and maintain economically self-sufficient households. The absence of public policies that reinforce Amber's right to stay home to care for a new child compromise Amber's health, the emotional, and economic stability of the household and the well-being of the children involved.

The inadequate laws and policies in the United States protecting the rights of children and families to be cared by one another results in the unnecessary vulnerability of parents, children, businesses, the economy, and society. Paid and protected family leave has increased the health of parents and children, lowered turnover costs for businesses, and boosted competiveness and productivity.

© Springer International Publishing Switzerland 2016
S. Gatenio Gabel, *A Rights-Based Approach to Social Policy Analysis*,
SpringerBriefs in Rights-Based Approaches to Social Work,
DOI 10.1007/978-3-319-24412-9_4

According to a recent International Labor Organization report covering 185 countries, there are *only two* countries among the 185 countries surveyed whose national laws do not include paid maternity leave—the United States and Papua New Guinea. The United States is the only high-income country that does not mandate paid leave for mothers. Nearly every member of the European Union (EU) provides at least 14 weeks of job-guaranteed paid maternity leave, during which workers receive at least two-thirds of their regular earnings (Addati, Cassirer, & Gilchrist, 2014).

There is a range in types of leaves, some of which overlap. The different leaves are defined in Box 4.1 and can be paid or unpaid. The leaves can offer support to

---

Box 4.1 Types of Maternal, Paternity, and Parental Leaves

Maternity leaves are job-protected leaves from work for employed women prior to birth and following childbirth (or adoption in some countries). In some countries the pre-birth leave is compulsory as is a 6–10 week leave following birth. In most countries, beneficiaries may combine pre- with post-birth leave.

Paternity leaves are job-protected leaves from employment for fathers that address gender equity. They are usually much briefer than maternity leaves and function as supplements to such leaves.

Parental leaves are gender-neutral, job-protected leaves from employment that usually follow maternity leaves and permit either men or women to share the leave or choose which of them will use it. If there is no specified maternity leave, a portion of these leaves is usually reserved for women, to ensure a period of physical convalescence and recovery after childbirth. Recently, in some countries, some portion of the parental leave is reserved for fathers, on a "use it or lose it" basis, to create an incentive for fathers to play a more active parenting role.

Child rearing leaves developed in some countries as a supplement to maternity leaves or as a variation on parental leaves. Longer than maternity leaves, sometimes not limited to parents with a prior work attachment, and paid at a much lower level, the benefit is often described as a kind of "mother's wage." In some countries the cash benefit may be the equivalent of the government subsidy for out-of-home ECEC and used either to supplement family income while one parent is at home or to purchase private care.

Family leaves are job- and benefit-protected leaves for working parents including maternity (birth or adoption), paternity, parental, child rearing, care for an ill child, time to accompany a child to school for the first time, or to visit a child's school, personal leaves. These leaves may be paid or unpaid. When paid, benefit is usually included in taxable income.

Source: Kamerman and Gatenio (2002). Mother's Day: More than Candy and Flowers, Working Parents Need Paid Time-Off. Columbia University, New York: Clearinghouse on International Developments in Child, Youth and Family Policies.

parents in two complementary ways: by offering job-protected leave after the birth or adoption of a child (meaning a parent can return to their job or a comparable one at the end of statutory allowed period away from work) and by offering financial support during that leave.

In the next section, the social issue, parental leave policy is situated through its history and purpose. The effects of the policy are briefly reviewed.

4.1 Situating the Social Issue

Nearly a century ago, maternity policies were enacted to protect the physical health of working women and their babies at the time of childbirth (ILO, 1919). In response to the dramatic rise in female labor force participation rates since the 1960s, many countries developed child rearing, paternity, and parental leaves to help parents manage working and family lives and also out of concern for child well-being. As working parents become the norm, these policies are increasingly important to promote maternal and child health and prevent discrimination against women in the workplace (ILO, 2010).

Maternity protection benefits enable women to combine their reproductive and productive roles and prevent unequal treatment in the labor force due to the reproductive role of women while promoting gender equality in employment. These protective measures include paid and unpaid leaves, prevention of exposure to health and safety risks before and after birth, breaks for breastfeeding, maternal and child health care services, and protection against discrimination regarding recruitment and dismissal (ILO, 2010).

Job-protected leaves following childbirth (and, more recently, adoption) have become the policy norm in almost all industrialized countries and are paid for through statutory sickness (temporary disability) benefits, unemployment insurance benefits, family allowance systems, employment benefits, or as a separate social insurance benefit. Largely beginning in the 1980s, countries established parental leaves as supplements to existing maternity leaves, extended leave policies with a view toward creating credible alternatives to out-of-home infant care, and made leave policies stronger instruments of gender equity. Today, 81 countries provide paid leave to new fathers either through paternity leave (specific to fathers), parental leave, or through some combination of the two (Heymann, McNeil, & Earle, 2013). In 60 of the countries, fathers are paid at least 75 % of their wages for at least part of the leave taken. Extended leave for fathers is far less likely—only 37 countries allow fathers the option of taking 14 weeks or more of paid time off (Heymann et al., 2013).

The benefits of maternal, paternal, and parental leave have been studied from the perspective of mothers, fathers, children, employers, relationships, society, and the economy in the United States and mainly throughout industrialized countries. A summary of research findings regarding the economic and the health and developmental benefits follow.

4.2   Economic Benefits of Leave Policies

Research on the benefits of leave to the economy, society, and employers presumes that the availability of leave increases labor force attachment of parents and as a consequence the workplace is more productive because higher retention reduces costs to employers, employee stress is lessened, and family income is more stable. Society benefits too because as a result of greater labor force attachment government spending on public assistance decreases, economic gain rises, the tax base expands, and consumer spending increases. Ruhm postulates that these benefits accrue because the availability of leave increases the likelihood that individuals who plan to use leave in the future will choose to work and has shown that female employment rates increase when paid leave is offered (Ruhm, 1998; Ruhm & Teague, 1995).

The lack of family friendly policies, such a maternal, parental, or paternal leave in the United States, is cited as one of the reasons that the ranking of the US female labor force participation rate dropped from 6th in 1990 to 17th in 2010 in the United States among the 22 Organization for Economic Co-operation and Development (OECD) countries (Blau & Kahn, 2013).

Not only are individuals more likely to work prior to children when paid leave is available, workers are also more likely to return to work post-childbirth thus increasing retention while reducing training costs and turnover. Hofferth and Curtin (2006) and Joesch (1997) found that women who were offered leave were more likely to return to work within the year than women who were not offered leave and to the same employer (Hofferth & Curtin, 2006). Berger and Waldfogel (2004) found that women with access to paid leave were more likely to take leave and stay home longer than women who did not have leave, yet women with access to leave were also more likely to return to the labor force after their period of leave than women who did not have leave.

Rossin-Slater, Ruhm, and Waldfogel (2011) found that paid leave enabled less advantaged women the ability to stay home financially and for longer periods of time. They also found that paid leave modestly increased the time spent at work once mothers return to work (2–3 h per week). Fathers too were more likely to take leave shortly after childbirth when paid leave was available (Baum & Ruhm, 2013).

According to Hofferth and Curtin (2006), even when leave is unpaid, women are more likely to return to their employers when leave is made available. Women in the United States who had a child after the enactment of the Family Medical Leave Act (FMLA) returned back to work more quickly than those who had a child pre-FMLA and were more likely to return to the same employer. Workers with low-skilled jobs were found that 82.7 % of employees in low-skilled positions were likely to return to their employers after taking available leave compared to 73 % of employees in similar positions who did not have leave (Appelbaum & Milkman, 2011).

Family leave policies increases productivity according to Meyer, Murkerjee, and Sestero (2001). In their study, the provision of work–family benefits was found to attract higher quality workers, reduce absenteeism and tardiness among employees, and reduce employee turnover—all contributing to higher productivity and profitability.

4.3   Health and Developmental Benefits of Leave

Research demonstrates that maternal and parental leave can enhance the health of mothers and children (ILO, 2010). The well-being of a mother, both emotionally and physically following childbirth can play an important role in the quality of care she is able to provide her child. Chatterij and Markowitiz (2012) report that mothers who take more than 12 weeks of maternity leave are less likely to report symptoms of depression, severe depression, and overall better health and mental health than mothers who take less than 3 months leave. Another study found that the longer leave taken by women post-birth (up to 6 months), the lower postpartum depression scores (Dagher, McGovern, & Dowd, 2014). Fathers' involvement in child caring increases when paid leave is available (Huerta et al. 2013). Fathers who take at least 2 weeks of leave carry out more child care activities during the first few months of their children's lives than fathers who do not take leave (Huerta et al. 2013; Nepomnayaschy & Waldfogel, 2007).

Research findings have linked breastfeeding to better health and mental health well-being of mothers and infants. Children who are breastfeed have strengthened immune systems (U.S. Department of Health and Human Services, 2000) and are at reduced risk of diarrheal disease, respiratory illnesses, ear infections, obesity, asthma, Type 2 diabetes, leukemia, and sudden infant death syndrome (U.S. Department of Health and Human Services, 2011). Breastfeeding can also increase mother and infant bonding and stimulate positive neurological and psychosocial development (U.S. Department of Health and Human Services, 2000). Maternity leave increases the likelihood of women breastfeeding (Berger, Hill, & Waldfogel, 2005). A study of California's Paid Family Leave program found that women who took leave breastfed twice as long as women who did not take leave (Appelbaum & Milkman, 2011). Another study that looked at the effects of Canada's policy change in 2000 that increased job-protected, paid maternity leave from approximately 6–12 months, found that women taking leave breastfed longer after the policy was expanded and were more likely to breastfeed exclusively for the recommended 6 months (Baker & Milligan, 2008).

There is some evidence that breastfeeding is beneficial to women's health as well. Breastfeeding is associated with reduced risks of breast cancer, particularly for women with a family history of breast cancer, ovarian cancer, and rheumatoid arthritis (Beral et al., 2002; Ip et al., 2007; Stuebe, Willett, Xue, & Michels, 2009).

Stuebe's study suggests that women who breastfeed for longer periods lowered the likelihood of having Type 2 diabetes (Stuebe et al., 2005).

Paid family leave is associated with lower rates of infant and child mortality, though causality has not been proven. In Heymann, Raub, and Earle's 141 country study (2011), countries with ten paid full-time weeks of maternity leave had nearly ten percent lower neonatal, infant and child mortality rates than those with fewer weeks leave. Tanaka (2005) showed a similar association between unpaid and paid leave and reduced mortality rates.

Berger et al. (2005) found that children in the United States whose mothers take at least 12 weeks of leave from work after childbirth are more likely to receive vaccinations and well-baby checkups during their first year of life. These results were confirmed by a comparative study of maternity leave across 185 countries that found the longer the leave, the higher the vaccination rates among children but when leave is not paid at a full-time equivalent level, the association of infant immunizations and leave weakens (Daku, Raub, & Heymann, 2012).

4.4   Availability of Leave

Despite research findings documenting the benefits of leave to parents, children and the economy, some 830 million women worldwide are not covered by adequate maternity protection. And even when leave policies exist in countries, there is considerable diversity, especially for parental leave regarding the length of leave, paid and unpaid and if paid benefit levels vary widely, flexibility in use (can leave be taken in blocks or part-time over what period of time), and whether leave is an individual or family entitlement (leave per parent or per family and transferability of leave among parents). In some countries parental leave is tied to early childhood education and care benefits.

In the European Union, all member states must provide at least 4 months parental leave per parent that can be transferable (European Commission, 2010/18/EU). The average number of weeks for parental leave is 86.9 among member states in the European Union (Schulze & Gergoric, 2015). This is in addition to the directive requiring 14 weeks of maternity leave for mothers in the period immediately preceding and following birth. In practice, however, European Union countries offer on average 23 weeks of maternity leave with the average compensation rate at 90 % of previous incomes (Schulze & Gergoric, 2015).

4.5   International Instruments and Laws

The United States is *not* party to several international human rights treaties that protect and promote the rights of mothers, parents, and including the Convention on the Elimination of All Forms of Discrimination against Women (CEDAW), the

International Covenant on Economic, Social and Cultural Rights (ICESCR), and the Convention of the Rights of Children (CRC). In fact the United States is the only country in the United Nations not to have ratified the CRC.

Do We Need Countries to Ratify Human Rights Treaties?

The nonratification of human rights conventions presents an interesting dilemma for casting a rights-based argument for countries. If human rights are universal, then should it matter whether a country has ratified a particular human rights instrument or not?

Following World War II, international organizations, sovereign states, transnational corporations, NGOs, international professional associations, and others have undertaken to develop global policies and institutional structures that promote human rights. The result is a growing body of international agreements, treaties, legal statutes, and technical standards, all rooted in the Universal Declaration of Human Rights (UDHR) that was adopted in 1948. Although only 30 articles in length and nonbinding, the UDHR is by any standard a powerful document. Part of its power and also its weakness is the boldness and ambiguity of its articles declaring our universal entitlements *not* to be subject to torture, inhuman treatment, arbitrary arrest, detention, and discrimination while guaranteeing the right to education, safety, thought, and governance. The fundamental rights declared in the UDHR are *unconditional* as written but in every country gender, poverty, class, and suspicion of alliances have restricted the application and realization of human rights.

Since the UDHR, there have been further elaborations of rights in subsequent covenants and treaties—and by now you are familiar with the critical ones such as CAT, CEDAW, CRC, CEFRD, CRPD, CRMW, and CPAPED. The principles of universality, indivisibility, interdependence set forth in the UDHR are reinforced in each of these subsequent treaties. Each of these subsequent treaties needs to be ratified by the country for it to become binding. In Chap. 2, customary international law was discussed. It refers to laws that are not legally binding yet are considered international obligations because of established state practice (Shaw, 2003). The UDHR could be considered customary international law and the subsequent treaties are elaborations of the UDHR.

If we accept this, then does a country need to ratify a specific convention to be held to the normative standards established in the treaty? What are the consequences of being held to standards that one has not signed onto through ratification? What might be some benefits of this approach?

Knowing that the United States has not ratified the major treaties that obligate duty bearers to provide parental benefits including leave, we nonetheless review the international human rights instruments to better understand how maternity, paternity, and parental leave benefits can be viewed and contextualized as a human right.

The following questions are posed: Is the right to maternity leave and benefits a human right in international human rights treaties? Are the rights to paternity and parental leave and benefits international human rights? Following this, a summary of domestic law in the United States regarding maternity, paternity, and parental leaves and benefits is presented.

4.6   Maternity Leave

Several international conventions explicitly state the right to maternity leave and protections including the ICESR, CEDAW, and the International Labor Organization Convention (ILO) No. 183. Article 10(2) of the ICESCR states, "Special protection should be accorded to mothers during a reasonable period before and after child-birth. During such period working mothers should be accorded paid leave or leave with adequate social security benefits." The ICESCR's Article 10 obliges governments to take appropriate measures to prevent discrimination against women due to maternity, to ensure their right to work, to provide social benefits for families to meet their obligations, and to protect pregnant women from harmful work practices and environments. This is reinforced by the United Nations Committee on Economic, Social and Cultural Rights General Comment that views the right to social security in Article 9 of the ICESR as including the obligation of a country to provide adequate maternity leave benefits and family and child supports (U.N. ICESR, 2008).

The right to maternity leave and protection is included in the CEDAW under Article 11. *Article 11(2)(b) of* CEDAW *requires States* "to introduce maternity leave with pay or with comparable social benefits without loss of former employment, seniority or social allowances" and Article 11(2)(d) obligates duty bearers "to provide special protection to women during pregnancy in types of work proved to be harmful to them." Article 12 calls on states to "ensure to women appropriate services in connection with pregnancy, confinement and the post-natal period, granting free services where necessary, as well as adequate nutrition during pregnancy and lactation."

The ILO Maternity Protection Convention (No. 183) adopted in 2000 recommends that all women be granted maternity leaves of no less than 14 weeks with adequate social assistance funds or cash benefits of not less than two-thirds of their previous earnings, that they receive medical benefits during that period, and that they be entitled to return to the same or an equivalent position at the end of the leave. Later the same year a nonbinding ILO recommendation urged states to extend maternity leaves to no less than 18 weeks followed by parental leave with accompanying cash benefits equaling the full amount of previous earnings and extending theses rights to adoptive parents (ILO Recommendation 191).

4.7 Paternity and Parental Leave

Unlike the right to maternal protection and leave that is explicit, the rights to paternal and parental leaves and benefits are implicit. The case for paternal participation in child caring benefits and leave is made on the basis of nondiscrimination, equity, and for the best interests of the child. As long as women continue to earn less than men for comparable skills, it can be argued that women continue to face discrimination in the workplace and that at least part of the discrimination may be due to the reproductive and primary caregiver roles women have assumed historically. Viewing women exclusively in these traditional roles have hindered women from full participation in work and public life. Changing these attitudes not only means treating women equally in the workplace, it also means allowing men to fully participate in family responsibilities in the home.

Support for this argument can be found in the UDHR, ICCPR, ICESCR, CEDAW, and the CRC. Article 2 of the UDHR declares that men and women are equal and are entitled to enjoy all rights set forth in the declaration without discrimination (Article 7). The International Covenant on Civil and Political Rights (ICCPR), one of the core international human rights treaties that the United States has ratified, also upholds these rights. Article 2(1) of the ICCPR states that all persons are equal before the law and are entitled to equal protection of the law without discrimination. The obligation of states to guarantee all persons equal and effective protection from discrimination can be found in Article 26 while Article 25 requires states to take measures necessary when the right of women to participate in public affairs is not fully equal (Håkansson, 2005). If women will be discriminated against in the workplace and public life because they are viewed as vehicles for reproduction and as primary caregivers, then in accordance with the ICCPR, providing maternity leave for women is insufficient to overcome discrimination. A country must also take steps to equalize caregiving roles within the family to conquer discrimination and equality.

Equity and nondiscrimination is repeated in the ICESCR in several places. Article 2 assures social, economic, and cultural rights without discrimination and Article 3 incurs states with the responsibility of ensuring the equal right of men and women to the enjoyment of all economic, social, and cultural rights. This state responsibility is further detailed in Article 6 regarding nondiscrimination and equal protection of employment. Article 7 requires states to identify and eliminate the underlying causes of pay differences.

CEDAW does not explicitly provide for paternal or parental leave; however, the commentaries leading to CEDAW are clear that contributing members believed that for gender equality to be achieved, child caring and other home responsibilities as well as work needed to shared equally (Håkansson, 2005). Several countries suggested that fathers be offered parental leave but there was a lack of consensus on this issue when CEDAW was being drafted (Håkansson, 2005). The CEDAW preamble emphasizes the social significance of both parents taking part in the upbringing of the children and for this responsibility to be shared between men and women and society as a whole. The preamble also states that men and women's traditional roles must change both in the family and in society, to achieve full equality. States are required to pursue all means without delay to eliminate discrimination against women under Article 2. Article 5 refers to changing social and cultural patterns of men and women toward equality and "the common responsibility of men and women in the upbringing and development of their children." It is Article 11 that expands on the state's responsibilities to eliminate discrimination for women at work particularly regarding childbearing, that state's are encouraged to provide "the necessary supporting social services to enable parents to combine family obligations with work responsibilities and participation in public life."

Parental leave and benefits have been considered from the perspective of a parent who holds the dual role of caregiver and employee. What about from the perspective of the child? Do children have a right to be cared for by their mothers and/or both parents? And if so, what is the state's responsibility in this regard? For this we look to the CRC. Article 5 of the CRC places the onus on governments to protect and assist families in fulfilling their essential role as nurturers of children. In the best interest of the child, Article 18 gives both parents the responsibility for raising children and instructs states to respect and support parental responsibilities, especially for working parents.

The right to maternity leave, job protection, and benefits are rooted in CEDAW, ICESCR, or the CRC—none of which the United States has ratified. However, given the availability of maternity leave and benefits in almost every other country in the world, maternity leave can be seen as customary practice around the world. The United States ratification of the ICCPR opens consideration of the right to paternal and/or parental leave on the grounds of equity and nondiscrimination (Article 26). If leave is only available to women, the role of women to care for children is reinforced and it is likely that employers will continue to discriminate against women in the workplace. This will also make it less likely for men who wish to take on greater roles within the home to be supported by employers. Arguably, given the support for parental leave in the CRC, ICESCR, and CEDAW and the ratification of the CRC by all countries but the United States and the ratification of the ICESCR and CEDAW by an overwhelming majority of countries around the world, suggests consideration of leave for both parents as customary international law (Håkansson, 2005).

4.8 Federal and State Laws in the United States

In contrast to other industrialized countries where the right to maternal, paternal, and/or parental protections and leave are part of national laws, the United States has a far looser and more complex system with fewer leave guarantees and benefits at the federal level. In this section, federal laws pertaining to maternal protection and family leaves are reviewed, consideration is then given to state laws and common practices.

4.8.1 Federal Laws

The Pregnancy Discrimination Act of 1978 (PDA) in the United States prohibits employers from discriminating against a woman because of pregnancy, childbirth, or a medical condition related to pregnancy or childbirth in the hiring, firing, pay, job assignments, promotions, layoff, training, fringe benefits (including leave, sick days, and health insurance), and any other term or condition of employment. The PDA does not require employers to provide paid leave or guarantee a women's job unless this is provided to other employees with a medical condition or temporary disability. The PDA was an amendment to the Civil Rights Act of 1964 to expand discriminatory practices to include sex discrimination on the basis of pregnancy. The Supreme Court ruled in 1976 that Title VII of the Civil Rights Act excluded pregnancy and 2 years later, the Civil Rights Act was amended by the PDA to include discrimination on the basis of pregnancy (Woods, 2012).

Prior to the passage of the Family and Medical Leave Act (FMLA) of 1993, the United States did not have a federal family leave policy. The formulation of leave policies was left to the states as well as the type of benefits offered and to whom (Kamerman & Kahn, 2001). There was a need for federal legislation because the PDA did not provide job-guaranteed leave and while many individual companies and some states offered some type of maternity, parental, or family leave benefits, leave policy was inconsistent and varied greatly.

The FMLA of 1993 allows eligible male and female employees in public and private agencies employing at least 50 workers to take job-protected leave for a serious health condition; to care for an employee's newly born, adopted, or foster child; or to care for an immediate family member with a serious health condition. Eligibility includes working for at least 1250 h in a year and having worked at least 12 months for their current employer. Almost 60 % of employees work at covered firms and met all eligibility requirements for FMLA benefits (Klerman, Daley, & Pozniak, 2013). Care leave is available to both mothers and fathers and can be taken for up to 12 weeks consecutively or in intervals throughout the year in whole or part days. While the FMLA does not require employers to provide pay, it does require employers to continue health insurance benefits during leave and allows employees to return to the same or equivalent job.

4.8.2 State Laws

Prior to the enactment of FMLA in 1993, several states already had some form of leave policy in place. Four states, Rhode Island, California, New Jersey, and New York, enacted temporary disability insurance (TDI) laws in the 1940s that provide cash benefits and cover pregnancy and post-childbirth. Puerto Rico and Hawaii followed in the 1960s. Most State TDI programs are funded by employee and/or employer contributions and pay up to 50–60 % of an employee's wage for up to 52 weeks of leave including disability due to pregnancy (Gault, Hartmann,

Hegewisch, & Reichlin, 2014). Women typically take 6–10 weeks of temporary disability leave for pregnancy, though they may take longer if their condition necessitates it according to state law. Leave under the TDI programs is based on health status resulting from pregnancy or childbirth. Fathers and adoptive parents are therefore ineligible for paid leave.

In addition to the TDI programs in the five states and Puerto Rico, states have introduced initiatives to provide workers with family job-protected leave and other benefits. Four states have established family leave insurance programs that provide partial wage replacement following the arrival of child or to care for an ill family member. California's Paid Family Leave (PFL) program extends its State Disability Insurance program to individuals needing time to care for a new or ill family members. PFL is funded through employee payroll taxes and provides about 55 % of wages (up to a maximum of $1095 in 2014) for up to 6 weeks. Employees who are eligible for the federal FMLA must take PFL concurrently. PFL does not offer job protection.

Similar to California's PFL, is the Family Leave Insurance program in New Jersey. Employees are eligible for up to weeks paid leave equal to two-thirds of wages (to a maximum of $595 per week) to care for a new or ill family member. It is funded through payroll taxes, must be taken concurrently with leave under FMLA and does not provide job protection for those not covered by the FMLA.

Rhode Island's Temporary Caregiver Insurance (TCI) program provides up to 4 weeks of wage replacement to care for a seriously ill child, spouse, domestic partner, parent, parent-in-law, grandparent, or to bond with a newborn child, newly adopted child, or new foster care child, with benefits. The cash benefit is a partial replacement of wages up to $770 per week and guaranteed job protection is included.

The state of Washington passed a Family Leave Insurance Law in 2007 that would provide a full-time worker with up to $250 per week for up to 5 weeks to care for a newborn or newly adopted child. The program has not been implemented because the funding mechanism is to be determined. In 2013, Rhode Island passed a law to expand its TDI program called "Temporary Caregiver Insurance (TCI)" that provides 6 weeks of paid leave. The program is similar to the California and New Jersey programs in that it is funded through a employee-only payroll taxes and provides partial wage replacement at the same rate as its TDI program (about 60 %) for new parents and other family caregivers by means of an employee-only payroll tax. Like Washington, the program has yet to be implemented.

In 13 states, the time period and/or coverage allowed under the FMLA has been extended, several states have included partial wage replacement, others have extended coverage to employees in public or private firms of less than the 50 employees covered by the FMLA (Winston, 2014). Vermont and San Francisco recently passed "right to request flexibility" laws requiring employers to consider employees' requests for different work arrangements (Winston, 2014). There is considerable variation across the states regarding who is covered, whether leave is paid or unpaid, duration of leave, benefit levels, and eligibility criteria regarding earnings and employment history. State and local government expansions include reducing the number of employees to become an eligible employer (i.e., Maine and

Table 4.1 Summary of types of leave in the United States

Policy area	Locus	Approach
Unpaid family leave	Family and Medical Leave Act (federal), state family leave laws (12 states), voluntary employer provision	Employer mandate
Paid parental/family leave	Temporary Disability Insurance (for mothers): CA, HI, NJ, NY, RI, Paid Parental/Family Leave (dedicated programs): CA, NJ, RI (effective January 2014), WA (not implemented), voluntary employer provision	Social insurance
Workplace flexibility	Right to request flexibility: VT, San Francisco. Some employer encouragement initiatives, voluntary employer provision	Employer mandate and employer voluntary

Source: Winston (2014)

Vermont expanded leaves to cover organizations of 15 or more workers), new definitions of family, and allowing leave to be used to attend activities related to children's well-being and domestic violence. Most state paid leave policies do not extend job protection benefits, leaving a gap between state and federal policy (Table 4.1).

In the United States, employers often have family leave benefits that go beyond the FMLA and state requirements. According to a 2013 Bureau of Labor survey, private employers report that at least 85 % of workers have some unpaid family leave (USDOL/BLS, 2013) but given the data on private firm provision varies depending on the survey and depending on the survey can overlap with other types of leave (e.g., sick leave, annual leave) (Winston, 2014).

Although the United States has not ratified the ICESCR, CEDAW, or CRC—all of which state view maternity leave as a human right, it has ratified ICCPR. This is important because the strong language in the ICCPR regarding nondiscrimination and equity can be used to make the case for paternal and parental leave. Gender neutrality has been used to further family policies in the United States, including the passage of the Pregnancy Discrimination Act and the FMLA (Woods, 2012). Though not legislated at the federal level in the United States, the majority of private firms offer some type of leave to care for a new child, suggesting that this has become common practice for employers to offer leave. It is time for domestic laws in the United States to catch up to common practices and realities of today's families.

4.9   Rights-Based Analysis of Maternity, Paternity, and Parental Leaves in the United States

Our analysis now turns to consider maternity, paternity, and parental leaves in the United States using the P.A.N.E. framework.

4.9.1 Participation

Family leave policies should strive to include those most affected by the policies in every stage of the policymaking process from identifying the social issue through evaluation of the program. In this case, representatives of working parents, especially mothers, should be active participants in determining family leave policies, as well as employers, children, and government representatives whose responsibilities include securing economic and health well-being for the country. Special consideration should be given to including the voices of low-income parents, single parents, and others who have historically been marginalized due to ethnicity, gender, language, or ability.

Securing evidence that the voices of these stakeholders were part of the policymaking process is a challenge. As a democracy, elected officials in the United States—at all levels of government—should represent the interests of their constituencies. Representing the multicultural, complex and wide-ranging and often conflicting interests of constituencies requires balancing many balls in the air simultaneously. We also need to understand how the stakeholders themselves participated in the making of policy around caring leaves.

Elving (1995) and Woods (2012) trace the policymaking process leading to the FMLA. In their accounts, the impetus for seeking a national, comprehensive, gender-neutral family leave bill came about in 1984 when California's maternity leave law was struck down by a federal district court as discriminating against men (because men were not offered comparable benefits). The court's decision led to a Californian elected officials meeting with representatives from the National Women's Law Center, Georgetown University Law Center, and Women's Legal Defense Fund. Following the meeting, a legislative proposal was drafted that became the basis of what eventually became the FMLA, which Representatives Howard Berman, Patricia Schroeder, William Clay and Senator Christopher Dodd, cosponsored.

From the beginning, the FMLA sought to protect women *and* men from losing their jobs when they became mothers or tended to other family caregiving responsibilities. Gender neutrality was important as a means of not diminishing the employability of women; not burdening women alone with caretaking responsibilities and building a strong legal standing for the policy on the basis of nondiscrimination (Elving, 1995; Woods, 2012).

In 1984, Ronald Reagan was the President, the Republicans controlled the Senate and the House of Representatives was under the control of the Democrats. To gain Democratic support, the cosponsors of the bill needed to muster support from the labor unions, which initially saw the leave bill as a "girl" bill and showed little interest. Labor's support was gained through the organizing efforts of women in the trade unions who presented it as a new labor standard issue concerning the balance of work and family. It was one of labor's top legislative priorities for Congress by 1991 (Elving, 1995).

The National Partnership for Women and Families, who then were known as the Women's Legal Defense Fund, took the lead in organizing a coalition to advance leave legislation from 1984. Among the broad-based coalition members were representatives from: women's groups including Business and Professional Women USA and the League of Women Voters; children's groups including the National PTA and the Children's Defense Fund; organized labor including unions ranging from the Service Employees International Union to the National Education Association to the United Steel Workers; senior groups such as the AARP and the National Senior Citizens Council; groups representing persons with disabilities like the Epilepsy Foundation and its network of parents of children with disabilities; professional groups including the American Academy of Pediatricians, the National Association of Social Workers, and the American Nurses Association; religious organizations, notably the Catholic Conference, the United Methodist Church and the Union of American Hebrew Congregations; and the business community including Businesses for Social Responsibility, Ben & Jerry's, Stride-Rite, and Fel-Pro, as well as Burlington Northern Railway and Control Data Corporation. The support from the Catholic Conference and the AARP were key in redirecting public opinion, arguing that leave was pro-family and avoiding competition among needs of young children vs. the elderly (Elving, 1995; Woods, 2012).

Public opinion research showed increasingly strong support for the FMLA during its 9 year journey toward enactment and thereafter (Elving, 1995). This was aided by published research demonstrating the positive effects of state leave laws and coalition building efforts within states (Elving, 1995; Woods, 2012). Still, as long as there was a Republican presidency and Republicans held control of the Senate, the bill's progress was halted despite efforts to move the bill forward in the House. The perceived potential negative effects of bill on business were the main reason for Republicans opposition. It was not until 1987 when the Democrats gained control of the Senate and Dodd took over as Chairmen of the Children and Families Subcommittee that hearings in Washington, D.C. and around the country were held on the proposed FMLA.

The FMLA did pass both houses in Congress and was sent to President Bush in 1991 and again in 1992. President Bush vetoed the bill twice. In 1992, the veto was overridden in the Senate (then controlled by the Democrats) but when it came to the House, the party line vote on the bill became evident and the House fell slightly short of the two-thirds majority needed to override a presidential veto. To woo support from Conservatives, the number of employees in a covered firm increased to 50, the number of weeks on leave was reduced to 12, and family relations eligible was limited to spouses, children, and parents. The business lobbies remained strongly opposed to the bill. Despite the leadership from Senators Dodd (Democrat, male) and Bond (Republican, male, Missouri) on the bill, support for the bill from males was not as strong as it was from female members of the House and Senate (Elving, 1995; Woods, 2012).

It was not until 1993 when Democrat Bill Clinton became President and the number of women increased in the Senate from three to six and from 29 to 48 in the House of Representatives, that the bill was passed. According to Woods (2012), there was a rush to get the bill passed because despite Clinton's support and the increased number of women in Congress, there was a decidedly Conservative orientation taking hold in Congress and the bill was rushed through (Woods, 2012).

By all expectations, the FMLA was seen as the beginning and bills to expand the FMLA were expected. Yet, the stumbling economy, the ensuing Conservative tilt in Congress and public opinion in the years after the enactment of the FMLA contributed to the FMLA staying unchanged. Since 1993, legislation has been introduced in more than half the states to pair the FMLA with paid leave or otherwise expand leave (Woods, 2012). Several states have moved forward and legislation was introduced in Congress after Obama assumed the presidency to implement paid leave. Efforts to move paid leave legislation forward, however, were stymied for some time by concern over the economy following the financial crisis among other issues that were priorities of the Administration and Congress.

The voices of key stakeholders in expanding family leave policies have played critical roles in moving forward and stalling legislation on leave-related policy. This group includes parents, families, women's groups, organizations representing children and their interests, religious groups, business groups, elected officials representing local and statewide constituencies, and at federal, state, and local levels. Politics and the economy have been important factors shaping the context for leave policies in the United States. Less active have been groups representing low-income parents and mothers, LGBTQ families, immigrant, and minority families, who historically have been marginalized in public policy making in the United States.

4.9.2   Accountability

As duty bearers, states have responsibility to implement laws, policies, and programs that further the realization of human rights in the country. Information should be accessible and decision-making processes should be transparent. Potential beneficiaries should have access to redress if they feel benefits have been wrongly denied in a timely manner and without repercussions.

Data on the provision and use of paid and unpaid maternity, paternal, parental, and other family leave in the United States is available through several data sources maintained by the federal government including the National Compensation Survey (NCS), the Survey of Income and Program Participation (SIPP), the American Time Use Survey (special supplement; ATUS), the 2012 Family and Medical Leave (FMLA) Survey, and the Current Population Survey (CPS). Each of these sources define parental leave differently, may have information on paid and/or unpaid leave, coverage, usage, and surveys employers or employees. As a result, survey results vary and portray different profiles of family leave provision and usage in the United States (Gault et al., 2014).

The survey results are widely available in published reports and on the internet. Information was not available about who accesses these reports but it stands to reason that low-income persons, persons with low levels of education, or low command of the English language are less likely to fully comprehend or utilize these reports or data results. Likewise, information on the consideration of leave policies into law or availability of leave and conditions is also likely to be less available to such persons.

Salaried workers and those with higher incomes are more likely to take family leave compared to hourly workers. This is largely due to the likelihood of leave, paid or unpaid, being more likely to higher income workers, and if unpaid, higher income workers are more likely to be able to afford to utilize unpaid leave (Phillips, 2004). Three recent and separate studies in California, New York, and New Jersey found that low-income women were less likely to be aware of the availability of leave (Houser & White, 2012; California Senate Office of Research, 2014; Community Service Society of New York, 2015). In New Jersey, about 60 % of residents were unaware of the State's Family Leave Insurance program and lack of awareness was most common among lower income nonwhites who were young, retired, or nonpartnered. In California, despite over a decade since the implementation of paid family leave and multilingual outreach campaigns, awareness of the program is low (California Senate Office of Research, 2014). Among low-income workers in New York, researchers documented the lack of information available about Temporary Disability Insurance (TDI), the New York City Pregnant Workers Fairness Act, and the Family and Medical Leave Act (FMLA) (Community Service Society of New York, 2015).

The U.S. Department of Labor's Employment Standards Administration enforces the FMLA. This agency investigates complaints of violations. If violations cannot be satisfactorily resolved, the department may bring action in court to compel compliance. A FMLA eligible employee also has the option of bringing a private civil action against an employer for violations. Each individual state has it own mechanism in place for resolving disputes under state extensions of family leave policy, which generally mimic federal procedures.

4.9.3 Nondiscrimination and Equity

A sate has the responsibility to ensure that leave laws, policies, and practice are nondiscriminatory and that priority is given to protect the most vulnerable segments of the population. Leave programs should be accessible to all persons including all parents, families, and children, especially those who have been marginalized due to family composition, race, ethnicity, sexual orientation, marriage, etc. One of the ways to understand discrimination and nonequity is analyze whether benefits from leave programs are accessible, available, and adequate to all persons.

The dramatic growth in the labor force participation of mothers in full-time employment in the United States has *not* been accompanied by changes in public policies to support efforts to balance work and family demands. Almost half of all children are raised in families where both parents work full time; this is higher for low-income families. Research findings indicate that significant disparities exist with regard to who has access to paid and unpaid leave by income, work status, education, race/ethnicity, and gender.

Higher salaried and wage-earning parents are more likely to take leave because leave is more likely to be available to them than to low-income parents (Winston,

2014). A U.S. Census Bureau study on patterns of maternity leave and employment from 1961 to 1995 found that workers combine formal maternity leave, paid sick days, vacation time, and other leaves available to them to maximize time off and income (Johnson, 2008). Higher income workers are more likely than low-wage workers to have the ability to piece together paid leave from these different sources and combine these with savings (Johnson, 2008). Lower wage workers are less likely to have accumulated sufficient savings and the absence of paid leave options makes it more likely that low-wage workers will not be able to take leave because their earnings from work are essential to the household (Lester, 2005). Blank, Behr, and Schulman (2001) found that workers with incomes below 200 % of the federal poverty line typically had no paid leave of any kind after the birth of a child.

Part-time workers are also less likely to take paid leave than full-time employees. Only 5 % of part-time workers have access to paid family leave and 77 % have access to unpaid family leave (U.S. Department of Labor, 2013) yet part-time working mothers were slightly more likely to take leave than full-time moms when it was available (46 vs. 42 %) (Laughlin, 2011) (Table 4.2).

Two-thirds of women in the United States with at least a bachelor's degree have access to some form of paid leave compared to 19 % of women without a high school degree (Laughlin, 2011). Another study looked at who took leave among those eligible for leave and found that 55 % of women with a college degree took paid maternity leave compared to 35 % of women with some college or only a high school degree and 25 % of women with less than a high school degree (Boushey, Farrell, & John Schmitt, 2013).

Access to leave also varies by race and ethnicity. Most striking is that Latinos have the lowest access to parental leave of any racial/ethnic group despite their being more likely to have young children in need of care or supervision. Nearly 60 % of Latino workers have children under the age of 18, compared to less than 40 % of white workers or black workers. Latino workers are also more than twice as likely as whites to have more than one child (Glynn & Farrell, 2012). And yet, one-quarter of Latino workers have access to paid parental leave compared to one-half of Whites, 47.6 % of Asians, and 43.3 % of Blacks (Glynn & Farrell, 2012).

Women more often are the leave takers. Men are less likely to take leaves for the arrival of a new child and when they do their leaves tend to be shorter than women's (Armenia & Gerstel, 2006). Interestingly, white men are significantly less likely to

Table 4.2 Access to leave and other supports in private industry jobs (2013)

Policy	Total (%)	Wages in bottom quartile	Wages in top quartile	Small business (<50)
Paid family leave	12	5	21	8
Unpaid family leave	85	78	92	76
Paid sick leave	61	30	84	50
Paid vacation time	77	49	91	66
"Flexible workplace"	6	1	15	4

Winston (2014)

take family leaves than white women and men and women of color (Armenia & Gerstel, 2006).

Much debate leading to the passage of the FMLA focused on gender inclusivity, especially nondiscrimination toward men. However, the unpaid nature of the leave reinforces two-parent, two-income households and traditional gender roles that implicitly suggest the mother will leave work to assume childcare responsibilities while being supported by their spouse. In the workplace, organizations tend to ignore the paternal roles in childcare compared to mothers' (Tracy & Rivera, 2010). Baum and Ruhm (2013) found that when leave is paid, the likelihood and time father's with take leaves increases.

4.10 Looking Forward

International human rights treaties such as ICESCR, CEDAW, and the CRC make clear that mothers have a human right to maternity leave with public supports. The ICCPR has been used to extend this right to fathers, claiming that providing mothers with paid leave and not to fathers is discriminatory and works against gender equity.

The United States ratification of the ICCPR is key to developing an argument for parental leave despite the United States' nonratification of the ICESCR, CEDAW, and the CRC. Discussions preceding both the passage of PDA and the FMLA in the United States centered on gender equity and nondiscrimination. In both cases, there was concern for discrimination against women in the workplace because of their reproductive roles and the potential for nonequitable benefits accrued to men because of their nonreproductive role.

Today, women are protected against dismissals in the workplace due to pregnancy and related conditions and both men and women in firms of 50 employees or more can claim unpaid, job-protected leave to care for a family member or themselves due to an addition to the family or health related matter. Women in five states are eligible for paid leave due to pregnancy and childbirth under public temporary disability insurance laws. In other states, parents are eligible for paid leave (though this is unlikely to be accompanied with job guarantees beyond FMLA). Perhaps most confusing and generous at the same time is the myriad of employer policies providing paid or unpaid leave of varying lengths of time, various pay levels, and eligibility criteria regarding length of employment, number of hours worked, and position. Parents often combine leaves to care for children with other types of leave such as vacation and sick days and rely on savings.

Because of the differences in how leave is defined in surveys and by employers, estimating the number of workers who have access to paid or unpaid leave to care for children often ends with a range. Nonetheless, it is clear that most workers in the United States have access to some kind of leave and employees who are white, better educated, and earn higher incomes are more likely to be eligible for leave than nonwhites, less educated, and lower wage workers.

As a result, despite the wide availability of leave, women take leave more often than men, and women with college or higher degree are more likely to take leave than women with high school degrees or less. White women are also more likely to take leave over other racial/ethnic groups. Among those least likely to take the leave are parents who work in firms of less than 50 employees (and are not covered by the FMLA), work less than full-time, earn less, and are lower skilled. This is inconsistent with Title VII of the Civil Rights Act of 1964, which forbids employment discrimination based on protected class status, and applies to employers with 15 or more employees. Lower income workers are disproportionately affected since they are not covered by the FMLA and smaller employers tend to pay lower wages and provide fewer paid benefits than employers covered by FMLA (Pesonen, 2015).

Going back to the ICCPR and domestic laws that uphold nondiscrimination and equity in the United States, it appears that current laws have resulted in inequitable results and reinforce discrimination regarding women in the workplace, unequal roles at home relating to child rearing between male and female partners, and further disadvantaging lower income earning parents and persons of color.

Lower income mothers are the least likely to have the option of leave because they are more likely to work fewer hours and at smaller firms. The voices of these women were not as prominent in the negotiations over the FMLA and are less likely to be represented by either labor unions or women's groups. Consequently, they are less likely to benefit equally from the current laws pertaining to leaves for parents to care for their children. Completely absent from most discussions on parental leave are the voices of low-income fathers. From a rights-based perspective, the principle of participation in decisions affecting their lives was violated by not having low-income parents fully participate in the negotiations. This omission and its effects call for a universal extension of the FMLA.

Though gender neutral, the FMLA needs to go further to promote gender equality. The United States ranks only 20th in the gender equity internationally (World Economic Forum, 2014). Strong parental leave policies can combat gender inequality in a manner similar to affirmative action; by recognizing and supporting parental needs regarding the balance between work, acknowledging the unique needs of men and women given their reproductive roles, providing incentives for men to take on greater responsibility in child rearing, promoting progressive policies to establish and maintain gender equality in the workplace and in the home.

Gender-neutral laws alone are unlikely to change longstanding sex stereotypes regarding work and family roles in our society. Laws need to motivate employers and parents to accept gender equality by rewarding fathers to take on new roles in the home including sharing child caring responsibilities and by changing the culture at work to reinforce fathers to take parental leave. Otherwise, society will default to sex stereotypes in determining how to balance work and family demands between men and women (Pesonen, 2015). Men's success as breadwinners is predicated on women's delegation to the homemaker role. The FMLA reinforces these roles because women are more likely to work less than full-time than men and earn less than men in settings that are less likely to offer paid leave or job-guaranteed leave.

Thus far, we have considered the rights of parents to leave to care for children based on a presumed model of a married, heterosexual couple. However, children are raised in a variety of family forms. Over two-fifths of all children were born to mothers who were not married thus raising the likelihood of children growing up with parents who are not married, divorced, or remarried. The majority of children in the United States will spend some of their childhood living in a single-parent or blended family home. The effects of current laws on same sex parents, married or otherwise, has not been but should considered as well as the equity of children being raised by persons other than parents, such as grandparents.

Until we achieve universal, paid and job-protected leave for all persons raising children, we will invariably discriminate or unfairly omit certain groups and in the process, thwart efforts toward the full realization of human rights for all.

The intent of this book and series is to stimulate thinking and discussion on how we redirect our professional practices, particularly in social work, toward standards that value human dignity and respect over efficiency. Far from complete, it is hoped that this will open discussions on better ways of achieving this goal that is at the root of our endeavors as social workers and has been a long time waiting.

References

Addati, L., Cassirer, N., & Gilchrist, K. (2014). *Maternity and paternity at work. Law and practice across the world*. Geneva: International Labour Office.

Appelbaum, E., & Milkman, R. (2011). *Leaves that pay: Employer and worker experiences with paid family leave in California*. Washington: Center for Economic and Policy Research. http://www.cepr.net/documents/publications/paid-familyleave-1-2011.pdf.

Armenia, A., & Gerstel, N. (2006). Family leaves, the FMLA and gender neutrality: The intersection of race and gender. *Social Science Research, 35*(4), 871–891.

Baker, M., & Milligan, K. (2008). Maternal employment, breastfeeding, and health: Evidence from maternity leave mandates. *Journal of Health Economics, 27*(4), 871–887.

Baum, C., & Ruhm, C. (2013). The effects of paid family leave in California on labor market outcomes, NBER Working Paper Series, Working Paper 19741.

Beral, V., Bull, D., Doll, R., Peto, R., Reeves, G., La Vecchia, C., et al. (2002). Breast cancer and breastfeeding: Collaborative reanalysis of individual data from 47 epidemiological studies in 30 countries, including 50,302 women with breast cancer and 96,973 women without the disease. *Lancet, 360*(9328), 187–195.

Berger, L., Hill, J., & Waldfogel, J. (2005). Maternity leave, early maternal employment and child health and development in the US. *The Economic Journal, 115*(501), F29–F47.

Berger, L. M., & Jane Waldfogel, J. (2004). Maternity leave and the employment of new mothers in the United States. *Journal of Population Economics, 17*(2), 331–349.

Blank, H., Behr, A., & Schulman, K. (2001). *State developments in child care, early education and school-age care 2000*. Washington, DC: Children's Defense Fund.

Blau, F. D., & Kahn, L. M. (2013). *Female labor supply: Why is the US falling behind?* Bonn, Germany: Institute for the Study of Labor.

Boushey, H., Farrell, J., & John Schmitt, J. (2013). *Job protection isn't enough: Why America needs paid parental leave*. Washington, DC: Center for American Progress and Center for Economic and Policy Research.

California Senate Office of Research. (2014). *California's paid family leave program: Ten years after the program's implementation, who has benefited and what has been learned?* Retrieved March 2015, from http://sor.senate.ca.gov/sites/sor.senate.ca.gov/files/Californias%20Paid%20Family%20Leave%20Program.pdf.

Chatterji, P., & Markowitz, S. (2012). Family leave after childbirth and the mental health of new mothers. *Journal of Mental Health Policy and Economics, 15*(2), 61–76.

Community Service Society. (2015). A necessity, not a benefit: NYC's low-income moms discuss their struggles without paid family leave and job security. Community Service Society of New York.

Dagher, R., McGovern, P. M., & Dowd, B. E. (2014). Maternity leave duration and postpartum mental and physical health: Implications for leave policies. *Journal of Health Politics Policy & Law, 39*(2), 369–416.

Daku, M., Raub, A., & Heymann, S. J. (2012). Maternal leave policies and vaccination coverage: A global analysis. *Social Science & Medicine, 74*(2), 120–124.

Elving, R. (1995). *Conflict and compromise: How congress makes the law.* New York: Simon & Schuster.

European Council Directive 2010/18/EU of 8 March 2010 implementing the revised framework agreement on parental leave concluded by BUSINESSEUROPE, UEAPME, CEEP and ETUC and repealing Directive 96/34/EC.

Gault, B., Hartmann, H., Hegewisch, J. M., & Reichlin, L. (2014). Paid parental leave in the United States: What the data tell us about access, usage, and economic and health benefits. Institute for Women's Policy Research.

Glynn, S. J. & Farrell, J. (2012). Latinos least likely to have paid leave or workplace flexibility. Center for American Progress. http://www.americanprogress.org/issues/labor/report/2012/.

Håkansson, E. (2005). Paternity leave as a human right: The right to paternity leave, parental leave for the father, as a way to actual gender equality in the view of CEDAW and other international instruments, Masters Thesis. Sweden: University of Lund.

Heymann, J., McNeil, K., & Earle, A. (2013). Filling a critical gap: Measuring work policies that affect families globally. *Community Work & Family, 16*(3), 239–260.

Hofferth, S., & Curtin, S. (2006). Parental leave statutes and maternal return to work after childbirth in the United States. *Work and Occupation, 33*, 73–105.

Houser, L., & White, K. (2012). *Awareness of New Jersey's family leave insurance program is low, even as public support remains high and need persists.* Center for Women and Work at Rutgers, The State University of New Jersey, Issue Brief, October 2012. Retrieved March 2015, from http://smlr.rutgers.edu/sites/smlr/files/FLI%20Issue%20Brief%20Final%20with%20Appendix.pdf.

Huerta, M., Adema, W., Baxter, J., Han, W-J., Lausten, M., Lee, R., & Waldfogel, J. (2013). Fathers' leave, fathers' involvement and child development: Are they related? Evidence from four OECD countries. *OECD Social, Employment and Migration Working Paper* No. 140, OECD Publishing.

International Labour Office. (1919). Maternity Protection Convention, (No. 3).

International Labour Office (ILO). (2010). *Maternity at work: A review of national legislation: Findings from the ILO database of conditions of work and employment laws.* Geneva, Switzerland: International Labor Organization.

Ip, S., Chung, M., Raman, G., Chew, P., Magula, N., DeVine, D., et al. (2007). *Breastfeeding and maternal and infant health outcomes in developed countries: evidence report/technology assessment.* Rockville: Agency for Healthcare Research and Quality, U.S. Department of Health and Human Services, AHRQ Publication No. 07-E007.

Joesch, J. M. (1997). Paid leave and the timing of women's employment before and after birth. *Journal of Marriage and the Family, 59*(4), 1008–1021.

Johnson, T. (2008). Maternity leave and employment patterns of first-time mothers: 1961–2003 *Household Economic Studies*, Current Population Studies, P70-113.

Kamerman, S. B. & Gatenio, S. (2002). Mother's Day: More than Candy and Flowers, working parents need paid time-off. Columbia University, New York: Clearinghouse on International Developments in Child, Youth and Family Policies.

Kamerman, S. B., & Kahn, A. J. (2001). Child and family policies in an era of social policy retrenchment and restructuring. In K. Vleminckx & T. M. Smeeding (Eds.), *Child well-being, child poverty and child policy in modern nations: What do we know?* (pp. 501–525). Bristol: Policy.

Klerman, J. A., Daley, K. & Pozniak, A. (2013). *Family and medical leave in 2012*, Technical Report, US Department of Labour (Washington). Retrieved April 2, 2014 from http://www.dol.gov/asp/evaluation/fmla/FMLA-2012-Technical-Report.pdf.

Laughlin, L. (2011). Maternity leave and employment patterns of first-time mothers: 1961–2008. U.S. Census Bureau.

Lester, G. (2005). Defense of paid family leave, *Harvard Journal of Law & Gender A, 28*, 1 http://scholarship.law.berkeley.edu/facpubs/645.

Meyer, C. S., Murkerjee, S., & Sestero, A. (2001). Work-family benefits: Which one maximizes profits? *Journal of Managerial Issues, 13*(1)

Nepomnayaschy, L., & Waldfogel, J. (2007). Paternity leave and fathers' involvement with their young children: Evidence from the American Ecls-B. *Community, Work and Family, 10*(4), 427–453.

Pesonen, A. (2015). Encouraging work-family balance to correct gender imbalance: A comparison of the Family and Medical Leave Act and the Iceland Act on Maternity/Paternity and Parental Leave. *Houston Journal of International Law, 37*(1), 158–196.

Phillips, K. S. (2004). Getting time off: Access to leave among working parents. Urban Institute.

Rossin-Slater, M., Ruhm, C. J. & Waldfogel, J. (2011). The effects of California's paid family leave program on mothers' leave-taking and subsequent labor market outcomes. NBER Working Papers 17715, National Bureau of Economic Research, Inc.

Ruhm, C. J. (1998). The economic consequences of parental leave mandates: Lessons from Europe. *The Quarterly Journal of Economics, 113*(1), 285–317.

Ruhm, C. J., Teague, J. (1995). Parental leave policies in Europe and North America. Working Paper 5065 (National Bureau of Economic Research, 1995), http://www.nber.org/papers/w5065.pdf?new_window=.

Schulze, E. & Gergoric, M. (2015). Maternity, paternity and parental leave: Data related to duration and compensation rates in the European Union. European Parliament: Directorate General for Internal Policies, Women's Rights & Gender Equality. Retrieved from http://www.europarl.europa.eu:studies.

Shaw, M. N. (2003). *International law* (5th ed.). Cambridge: Cambridge University Press.

Stuebe, A. M., Rich-Edwards, J. W., Willett, W. C., Manson, J., & Michels, K. (2005). Duration of lactation and incidence of type 2 diabetes. *Journal of the American Medical Association, 294*(20), 2601–2610.

Stuebe, A. M., Willett, W., Xue, F., & Michels, K. (2009). Lactation and incidence of premenopausal breast cancer, a longitudinal study. *Archives of Internal Medicine, 169*(15), 1364–1371.

Tanaka, S. (2005). Parental leave and child health across OECD countries. *Economic Journal, 115*(501), F7–F28.

Tracy, S. J., & Rivera, K. D. (2010). Endorsing equity and applauding stay-at-home moms: How male voices on work-life reveal aversive sexism and flickers of transformation. *Management Communication Quarterly, 24*(3). http://mcq.sagepub.com/cgi/content/abstract/24/1/3.

U.N. Committee on Economic, Social and Cultural Rights (CESCR). *General comment no. 19: The right to social security (Art. 9 of the Covenant)*. Retrieved February 4, 2008, E/C.12/GC/19.

U.S. Department of Health and Human Services. (2000). HHS blueprint for action on breastfeeding. Washington, DC: U.S. DHHS, Office of Women's Health. Retrieved from http://www.cdc.gov/breastfeeding/pdf/bluprntbk2.pdf.

U.S. Department of Health and Human Services. (2011). *The surgeon general's call to action to support breastfeeding*. Washington, DC: U.S. Department of Health and Human Services, Office of the Surgeon General.

U.S. Department of Labor, Bureau of Labor Statistics. (2013). National compensation survey: 2012 employee benefits in the United States, March 2013. Tables 16, 32, and 40. Bulletin 2776, September 2013. Retrieved from http://www.bls.gov/ncs/ebs/benefits/2013/ebbl0052.pdf.

Winston, P. (2014). Workforce supports for low-income families: Key research findings and policy trends. U.S. Department of Health and Human Services, Office of the Assistant Secretary for Planning and Evaluation.

Woods, D. (2012). *Family policy in transformation*. UK: Palgrave Macmillan.

World Economic Forum. (2014). The Global Gender Gap Report 2014. World Economic Forum.

Made in the USA
Middletown, DE
16 May 2018